DATE DUE			

AN INTRODUCTION
TO THE
WORLD OF CHILDREN'S BOOKS

To the five children who people my personal world
Moray, Tim, Avril, Richard and Ron jun.

AN INTRODUCTION
TO THE
WORLD OF CHILDREN'S
BOOKS

Margaret R. Marshall

A Grafton Book
Gower

Published by
Gower Publishing Company Limited
Gower House
Croft Road
Aldershot
Hants GU11 3HR

028.55
M35i
12 8461
ayn. 1984

ISBN 0 566 03437 9

Printed and bound in Great Britain by
Biddles Ltd, Guildford and King's Lynn

Contents

Introduction

A book about the world of children's books may suggest, to the person new to the subject, a simple account of the popular or classic literature for children, but the children's book world is not simple nor concerned only with books. It is a complex structure of the written word, the illustrated idea, the psychology, sociology and education of children and their aesthetic values and the even more complex attitudes and values of the adults who concern themselves with children and books.

The children's book world is affected by geography, language, politics, religion, economics, communications and social patterns of living. Even the phrase 'children's books' is deceptively simple.

The term 'children' covers young people in the First, Second and Third Worlds and those in the Fourth World, the children of seafarers, prisoners, refugees and gypsies. Then there are children in boarding schools and in comfortable homes; children in inner cities and children in prosperous farming areas; children in isolated mountain or desert areas; children with plenty to eat and children who are starving; children who are child prostitutes and children who live very sheltered lives; children who are handicapped mentally, visually, aurally, physically, some or all of these; children who are black, white, brown, mixed; children of different and differing religions; children who are male or female; children who are married or single; children who see war on television, children who live in war-torn countries and children who are fighting in wars; children who have food, health, education and love, and children who have none.

When I use the term 'children' in 'children's books' I see each and every one of these. When I use the word 'literature' or 'books', I mean those forms of reading material prepared for, offered to and read by children, other than the texts specifically intended to teach the mechanics of reading and those works covered by the term 'textbook'.

In countries with a high level of illiteracy there tends to be a concentration on publishing educational reading texts rather than children's literature and perhaps this is a necessary priority, in that children must first learn to read and be educated, but it is a priority which produces children technically able to read but with no pleasure or leisure reading material in the form of enjoyable stories with which to exercise the skill.

In some countries children's books are not considered important and therefore writers do not write for children. The bi-lingual and multi-lingual nations have special problems in this matter; for example Singapore's Educational Publications Bureau set up by the Ministry of Education produces local language material mainly of an educational nature but there is a heavy reliance on importing books in the four languages spoken in Singapore, Chinese, Malay, Tamil and English, most of which are of little relevance to the experience and culture of children in Singapore.

Spanish–American literature is a new literature and is helping to give an understanding of the social and cultural heritage in addition to its role as a means of reading enjoyment for leisure. But in all countries, only when there is official recognition of the importance of children, their education, literacy and their reading needs will there be a market for children's books. This will encourage publishing houses to set up, which will provide a channel for authors and illustrators and stimulate them to write for the child population.

As book production costs increase, as populations grow in

some countries and decline in others, as public expenditure is curtailed and private expenditure has to reconsider its priorities, there is a danger that the food for the mind that is contained in books will not be grown in the field of book production nor will be allowed to lie unharvested by those who reap on behalf of the child reader.

This book is intended for those who are new to the field of children's books, or who are already in it but need to have an overview or to see their part in perspective.

In the nearly thirty years I have spent in the world of librarianship, education and books I have worked in Britain, the West Indies and West Africa, visited twenty-one countries and met many librarians and teachers who are working with children but who have not studied children's literature nor, in many cases, undertaken education or training in librarianship. Practices may differ from country to country in publishing, marketing, education and library provision but books for children tend to follow a similar pattern because they satisfy similar needs world-wide.

Although many of the book examples are of British publications, the information about the genre is in most cases of international application, and the emphasis throughout the book is on the wider perspective of the children's book world.

I acknowledge the help of the following; the libraries of the National Book League and the Library Association in London and of the International Youth Library in Munich. I acknowledge Unesco's Division of Book Promotion for permission to reproduce the table of children's book publishing statistics.

Margaret R. Marshall
Oct. 1981

CHAPTER ONE

Trends in the Children's Book World

The world of children's literature is noticeably dominated by the large quantity of British and American children's books, but there are indications of growth in a number of countries, mostly related to the kinds of social and technological developments that helped to produce the first golden age of children's literature in the late nineteenth and early twentieth centuries in Britain.

The breaking down of international barriers, the movement of populations, the increase in literacy, the invention of technical processes applicable to book production, have all influenced recent trends. One of the most important developments is the spread and interchange of children's books across national boundaries by means of translation.

Translations

For many years the small-language European countries have translated English and American books in order to increase the quantity of literature available for their children. Recently other European countries have begun to translate English language books into German, the Scandinavian languages, Italian and Spanish. They have also increased the quantity and range of their own publications for children, particularly in the socialist bloc countries, and some of these works have been translated into English, German and Russian.

In some countries, both developed and developing, there are no children's books written by indigenous authors in the vernacular, and no books translated into the language or languages of the country. These children may read, if they can, the imported books. One example is Benin, formerly Dahomey, in West Africa, where French is the official language and Gung and Fon the major indigenous tongues.

Some countries have a small amount of local publishing for children and a large programme of translation. For example it is common to find in Egypt and Libya, simple books from Britain and Russia translated into Arabic. Small-language countries like Norway and Holland both with excellent indigenous writers, find it necessary to carry out translation of English language books in order to provide the quantity of books necessary for children's choice in reading.

The need for translation in such countries lies in the lack of indigenous books which may be the result of political, social or educational factors, or simply, as in the small-language countries, too small a market in that language to make publishing a viable concern.

But there is another need for translation, that exemplified in Britain, the USA and the USSR, all producing a large amount of children's literature annually. This need is for a widening of knowledge and culture, a receiving rather than a giving. So rich has been the children's literature of those countries that there has been no felt need to import much from other countries in the past. Some 'foreign' books have found their way into British children's hearts over the years, such as Louisa May Alcott's *Little Women* and Mark Twain's *Huckleberry Finn*, from the USA, with more recently, the works of Betsy Byars, Paul Zindel and Virginia Hamilton. From France came Perrault's tales, Babar and Madeline; from Germany Grimm's tales, Emil, and more recently Christine Nöstlinger's books; from Scandinavian countries came Hans Christian Andersen's tales, Pippi Longstocking, Mimff, Moomin and more recently, the wealth of teenage

11

novels, and books about children with problems and handicaps; from Netherlands Britain has benefited by the works of Biegel, Bruna, Andreus, Reesink and Rutgers van der Loeff. From Japan have come the works of, for example, Mitsumasa Anno and Satomi Itchikawa. The American multi-cultural society, the result of years of world-wide immigration, has produced a rich picture of the world in children's books from its immigrant authors, but has also recently embarked on systematic programmes of translation of the works of writers who still live in their native lands.

For the first time there is international recognition of the importance of sharing each other's literature. This is closely bound up with:

1. Producing a literature for children
2. Preserving that literature
3. Researching that literature

In order to do items two and three there has been a recent strengthening of the belief that each country should have a national centre for children's literature, from which should then follow encouragement and help to authors in producing item one, a children's literature.

National centres for children's literature
The International Youth Library in Munich has long had the function of collecting and preserving and promoting knowledge of the world's literature, under its director Walter Scherf, while other centres have had a national function, for example, the Swedish Children's Book Institute and the Library of Congress Children's Book Center. It is ironic that Britain which produces so much children's literature and has such a developed network of libraries, literary criticism and promotion of children's books, does not have a national centre. There are several agencies undertaking the various functions between them but without national co-ordination,

such as the British Library which collects children's books under the legal deposit system, the National Book League which preserves some children's books, provides information, and promotes the books through booklists, exhibitions and advice, the Victoria and Albert Museum which has collections of rare and early and representative children's books, and, throughout the country there are special collections held by libraries and individuals. Research in children's literature is done by individuals and university departments, but despite repeated pressure from groups of authors, librarians, publishers and readers, the finance and reorganization needed for a British centralized agency have not been forthcoming.

In recent years IFLA (International Federation of Library Associations) has set up the Round Table of Librarians of Documentation Centres Serving Research in Children's Literature, and members include such libraries as:

Library of Congress, Washington
National Library of Canada, Vancouver
La Joie par les Livres, Paris
Netherlands Centre for Public Libraries and Literature, The
    Hague
Biblioteca Nacional, Madrid
Swiss Children's Literature Institute, Zurich
Swedish Children's Book Institute, Stockholm
Banco del Libro, Caracas
South Australia State Library, Adelaide
Denmark Pedagogical Library, Copenhagen
Juvenile Literature Institute of Finland, Jyvaskyla
Kerlan Collection, University of Minnesota
Boys and Girls House, Toronto
International Youth Library, Munich

It can be seen from these examples that children's book

institutions with some kind of national function fall into the following categories:

1. A special section within a national library
2. A children's book specialist within a national or state library
3. A section within an education library
4. A university institution
5. An independent children's book institution or library.

Some of the common functions of these centres, whether developing or long established, include promoting and supporting both the ideals and practice of research in children's literature at national and at international levels; providing access to and preserving collections of children's books and related materials; compiling and maintaining bibliographical information; materials and advice for users and enquirers.

The same influences that have produced the increase in translation, and the setting up of centres for children's literature and for research, have also had their effect on the population. In this respect one particular trend, world-wide, is that towards considering the book needs and rights of ethnic and language minorities.

Multi-ethnic, multi-cultural and multi-lingual aspects
The rise in interest in books for minority language and immigrant peoples is the result of a number of factors, for example:

1. Oppression or war, causing an outflow of refugees to neighbouring or other countries.
2. Poor economic conditions which influence people to go as guest workers or as migrants to other countries.
3. The recognition that second and third generation children of the original migrants may have identity/language/education/employment problems.
4. The move towards wider state control has caused some

small-language groups (often with a long history and strong culture within their own country) to make their presence felt, backing their demands with the human rights argument of the right to their language and to read in their language.

5. The growth of research into all kinds of children's literature.

Examples of these trends can be seen in the increased translation in Russia of children's books into the approximately sixty languages of the USSR and satellite states. Elsewhere there is demand for children's books in Catalan, Welsh, Basque and Esquimaux by the inhabitants of their areas. There is a trend towards special library attention to the children of immigrants and minority groups in the USA, such as Puerto Ricans, Chinese, Europeans and North American Indians. In Britain the special language groups include for example Bangladeshi and Indians (Urdu, Hindi, Gujerati languages), Italians, Maltese and Vietnamese, and Welsh-speaking children. In Germany the children of Turkish guest workers require books and in Australia there are large numbers of Turkish, Greek and Yugoslav migrants needing their own language material in addition to simple English language books.

These particular language and cultural needs help to internationalize and cross fertilize children's literature by increased original material in minority languages; by increased translation of the world's literature; by increased provision of migrant language material; and by introducing the adopted country's literature to the migrant people.

While African, Asian and South-East Asian countries have many vernaculars within their state borders, often with no written literature in the vernacular, those that have a published literature know that many of their people are illiterate. There is a difference between the small-language minority groups in their own country and the small ethnic minority groups in an adopted country in terms of literacy, availability of material and interest in native language reading. However, trends show that the former group is concerned with keeping its language alive by publishing and by using it in education, while the latter group is more concerned about literacy in both the native language and the newly adopted country's language.

Multi-ethnic literature is being published to cater for multi-ethnic or multi-cultural societies and this is reflected also in the changing content of books for children and young people.

The changing content of books for children
Throughout the world of children's books many countries have shown a marked increase in the production of books with social realism as the main content. This is particularly noticeable in Italian, Danish, Swedish and American books, followed closely by British books. To some extent this is linked with the growth of that genre known as the teenage novel where social, emotional and sexual realism can be found, and this is covered in more detail in Chapter Five. But books for younger children also cover themes of identifiable realism.

This has come about partly because of the fact that in many Western countries children no longer lead the sheltered lives common to earlier generations. Not only are they taught about the wider social, political, cultural and personal aspects of life, but in those countries where television is common much is learned from watching a variety of programmes, even in countries where television is a political instrument of the state. There is too, amongst some writers, publishers and educators, the belief that children *should* know about subjects previously taboo, and that realism has as much right to a place in children's literature as has magic and fantasy. This belief is discussed in Chapter Five.

The enrichment of the population by the immigrant communities has meant a reflection of the multicultural society in themes, in characters and in illustrative content in children's books, and this has been emphasized in Britain by a publisher-sponsored annual award (Collins) for a children's book which reflects life in multi-ethnic Britain.

Controlling the content of children's books

A trend which is being strongly pursued by some people is the attempt to exclude, delete or ban from children's books, references to what are considered to be sexist, racist, politically unfavourable, or religious themes, comments or characters. This is covered more fully in the section in the chapter on selection, but must be mentioned here as two separate lines of discussion.

The first is the laudable desire to give humans of whatever race, colour, religion, sex or political viewpoint, their rightful dignity by *encouraging* writers to write positively on these issues. The second line is, to me and many others, the disturbing development, that there are those who believe (a) that all books already written should be examined for signs of these issues and banned if considered guilty by the banners' criteria; (b) that all writers must adhere to a code of practice which would, for example require a writer to balance a 'bad' character or situation with an obligatory 'good' one; (c) a politically motivated belief that children's books must be used to show children how oppressed they are by parents and authority and how anarchy can be achieved. (This aspect is common to a number of European countries.)

There have developed in several countries pressure groups of both the right and the left, and of women's rights, children's rights, nationalists and others, which seek to influence past, present and future literature for children. The propagandist, didactic approach which seeks to erase the

17

'unacceptable' history and to allow only the 'acceptable' present and future is a dangerous trend, to be countered.

Visual content

Linked with changing content is the change in visual content. This is covered in more detail in the section on children's book illustration but here includes the developments in illustrative content brought about by the technological changes in colour printing and book production, which have given more freedom to illustrators in both fiction and non-fiction. Czechoslovakia, Holland and Japan are strong influences here.

Apart from the styles and methods of illustration the outstanding innovation is the use of photographs which though long in use in British and American children's picture and information books, has recently opened up the information book scene in many European countries.

The reasons for increased attention to the visual aspects lie not only in the technological ability to experiment, which has produced magnificent examples of art books, picture strip art, pop-up and paper engineering in recent children's books, but in the social influence of television in those countries where children have access to it. The appeal of television to the visual sense is such that children are being conditioned to expect visual information and pleasure from other media, and that includes books.

It is perhaps a sign of the trend, at least in Britain, that the promotion of books via television is effective both with children and with children's librarians. There are at the time of writing three children's book programmes on television in Britain. These are in addition to the daily *Jackanory* storytelling programme the daily reading of children's stories in pre-school programmes and in schools broadcasting on television, the occasional coverage of children's books, children's book authors or children's book issues, which are included in the regular book discussion programmes for adults, the serialization of children's books in drama form, and the showing of filmed children's books from time to time on television.

The three programmes are: The BBC's *The Long, the Short and the Tall*, a series of programmes which recommends children's books by means of read excerpts, films of the story, talking with the author and with children about particular books, hosted by Aidan Chambers and Grace Hallworth, screened mid-evening and aimed at adults more than children. The second is Yorkshire Television's *Book Tower*, a series of programmes for children in which a well known actor, Tom Baker, recommends children's books by similar means, screened late afternoon. The third example is *Smith and Goody*, a series for children, screened early evening in which two comedy actors talk to each other in a humorous way about specific books and act out characters or plots, generally behaving in a thoroughly slapstick way, with very forthright comments on whether they like or dislike a book. It is very much directed at children who do not like reading but is fun also for those who do.

In the USA the CBS-owned and operated television stations started in 1981 a six-month project called *Eye on Reading*, consisting of a 60-second commercial dramatizing a scene from a children's book. At an exciting point the announcer told the viewer to find out what happened by reading the book, available from library or bookshop. Thirty books were selected for the project by specialists from the ALA and the International Reading Association.

In both the US and British examples viewers can send for a list of the books mentioned on the programme and children's librarians and bookshops are alerted to the need to be ready for children asking for the books they have seen on the programmes.

Summary
Trends do not normally develop independently; they are usually the culmination of a series of activities or events.

The recognition of the internationalism of children's literature comes after a period of the gradual recognition of the rights and needs of children, normal or handicapped, largely through the work of the United Nations agencies. Other factors include:

1. The breaking down of national barriers through increased travel, television, communication by satellite, which in turn causes the child of one country to be more familiar with the life of a child in another country, and therefore more able to appreciate its literature.
2. The development of printing processes and the use of high technology in book production causing global interest, mass production and new possibilities of physical format.
3. The movement of import and export trading into some countries previously isolated or unexplored commercially, books forming a part of that trading.
4. The development of national pride in their heritage in many countries formerly conquered, colonized or undeveloped, creating an interest in the traditional tales and literature.
5. Increasing literacy which has produced adults who now write and, currently, children who now read.
6. The development of library service to children and the growth of specialization in school and children's library staffing.
7. The growth in opportunity to study children's literature whether at a school of librarianship, in education for teachers, or at university or college as part of the study of a nation's literature. These in turn have led to

8. An increase in the number of children's literature specialists, who have banded together in local, national and international organizations concerned in one way or another with children's literature to write it, publish it, sell it, identify it, research it, judge it, teach it, promote it, preserve it and supply it to children.

Further readings

Chambers, Nancy ed. *Signal Approach to Children's Books*. London, Kestrel, 1980

Gersom, Diane ed. *Sexism and Youth*. New York, Bowker, 1974

Issues in Children's Book Selection. New York, Bowker, 1974

Ray, Colin. comp. *Background to Children's Books*. London, National Book League, 1977

Tucker, Nicholas. *Suitable for Children?* Brighton, Sussex U.P., 1976

CHAPTER TWO

What is Children's Literature?

Literature for children, whether it is fiction or non-fiction, is part of the larger world of literature and can be written, read, studied, analysed, taught and promoted in the same way as literature for adults, or any other age or subject group.

In the same way as for adult literature it can be broken down into categories by form, into for example hardback, paperback, tape, picture book, junior novel, teenage novel; into fiction which can be subdivided into historical, animal, adventure, science fiction, fairy, school stories, humorous, social, and many other broad themes for story. It can be divided into series, sequels or into national categories such as English, American, Indian, African, German, Australian, Scottish or Japanese children's literature and it can be further subdivided into age groupings such as 0–5, 6–8, 9–12, 13–19 or by reading ability groupings.

These are all external labels applied to certain texts and/or illustrations, but what are the factors which have caused the interested adult to pick out from literature in general those books that speak particularly to the minds and interests of children and young people?

1. Is there a kind of writing specifically suitable for children?
This raises educational constraints. The term 'suitable' often means different things in different countries. In many Western countries it may mean morally suitable in the sense that certain themes are considered to be taboo in order to protect children from those aspects of adult life thought to be corrupting, unpleasant, or sexual. 'Suitable' may also refer to

the educational relevance. Perhaps the book may be thought to cover a theme, or be written in a style, that children cannot understand until a certain stage of mental, physical or reading development has been reached.

But there are many countries where 'suitable' books for children are achieved by requiring them to reflect the political, social or religious outlook of the State. This often produces books that can be called didactic, meaning, intended to teach or to be instructional. Didacticism is a word frequently found in writings about children's books in many countries, particularly in the early years of English children's literature. But these aspects are looked at in more detail in Chapter Eight.

2. *Is there a literature aimed at children and therefore, by implication, not for reading by adults?*

This is even more arguable and makes it necessary to distinguish between books written *for* children and books *read* by children, and between books written for adults and books read by adults. Experience shows that in most countries where children are literate there is no rule which says that children cannot or must not read books supposed to be for adults, or vice versa.

There are numerous examples in English literature of books which are read and enjoyed by adults and children alike, such as *Alice in Wonderland* and *Winnie the Pooh*, both of which offer greater depths to the adult reader than to a child reader. Similarly from English 'adult' literature so-called adult books like Tolkien's *Lord of the Rings* and L. P. Hartley's *The Go-Between* attract young readers also.

The myths and legends whether read from books or heard via the storyteller are enjoyed by adults and children in every country.

Some writers say that they write for themselves rather than for an age group of reader, but other writers do have a child or a range of children in mind when they are writing a book, and they try to tailor the concepts, events and the vocabulary for that readership. In both cases some of the resulting books cross the very blurred dividing line between a book for children and a book for adults. So the author's aim or lack of it does not necessarily create a children's book. Children and adults read across whatever boundaries are made by publishers, librarians, teachers or parents.

3. *Is children's literature a lower level of writing, a second best training ground for writers who will then progress to writing for adults?*

This suggests that children are less intelligent than adults instead of simply knowing less than adults. Many writers of books write both adult and children's books. Some start with adult fiction or non-fiction and later write a book for children, others start with a children's book and then write for the adult market. Many alternate between the two over the years. Investigation of this aspect amongst established writers, past and contemporary in the English speaking world, would reveal that the great majority of authors of children's books also write adult books.

Many writers and illustrators say that children's literature requires much more research, attention to detail and careful writing for the text and art work, though there are of course many examples of second rate writing and illustration. In most countries children's books can be found in which it is obvious that little is expected of children and little is offered them.

Simplicity does not mean second rate. There are many simple books for young children and older less able children which are very well thought through by the author, illustrator, designer and publisher. Equally there are many lengthy prose works which turn out to be examples of books in which the authors have not given sufficient thought to plot, style, characterization and vocabulary. So the length of the book and the density of the writing must not be equated with quality.

4. *Is one of the distinguishing factors that the characters in the books are children?*

Some of the best known characters in literature confound this. Cinderella and Sleeping Beauty were past puberty; Big Claus and Little Claus and Ali Baba were adult baddies; Robin Hood, King Arthur, Pandora and Persephone were all adults; in fantasy fiction C. S. Lewis's Aslan, Tolkien's Hobbit, Grahame's Badger, Ratty and Mole are all adults in symbolized form, as are Anansi and Brer Rabbit. Most of Leon Garfield's characters are adult, so are Rosemary Sutcliff's. Mrs. Pepperpot, Mary Poppins, Raymond Briggs' Father Christmas and Fungus the Bogeyman are adults, as are Beatrix Potters's Mrs. Tiggywinkle and the people who live in Charles Keeping's *Railway Passage*. Most of the characters in the world's myths and legends were adults.

But there are many books which do have child characters and the good books relate the plot to the child's experience. In some cases it is an adult's view of a child's experience and, sometimes, an adult's view of what he thinks a child's experience ought to be. Child characters as such, are not necessarily a distinctive factor unless shown in relationship to the adult world or adult behaviour patterns, neither is child experience in terms of the so-called 'realistic' description of social setting or patterns of behaviour. This can be limiting to both writer and reader whereas the child's experience of *emotion* tends to be the same as an adult's. It may be much more intense because the child has not yet learned to control the emotions, and the emotion may pass more quickly because new experiences are crowding into a child's life at a fast rate. But books built upon the emotional aspects of the theme can cross national frontiers better than those based on a fixed time or place.

The experience of emotion and the description of social and emotional realism seem to come together most obviously in the genre of fiction known as the teenage novel, and this is looked at in more detail in Chapter Five. Although the presence of a child character may not make the book a children's book the author's characterization of the child's emotions is a crucial factor.

5. *What about language as a characteristic of children's literature?*

There is a common belief that for children, language, vocabulary and sentence structure involve writing 'down' by choosing simple words and shortening sentences to aid understanding. In picture books for the young child and for the retarded reader of any age this may be necessary. For these there are usually illustrations to give clues to the words in the text. But the writers who make concessions to vocabulary or structure unrelated to the theme of the book (unless it is for a 'special' readership), are likely to produce superficial and undemanding books. Short simple words and sentences can be rich, as in the first page of Ted Hughes' *Iron Man*.

> The Iron Man came to the top of the cliff. How
> far had he walked? Nobody knows. Where had he
> come from? Nobody knows. How was he made?
> Nobody knows.

Short simple sentences are effective in many of the myths, legends and folk lore tales, as in the story of *How Saynday Got the Sun*, from *North American Legends* edited by Virginia Haviland.

> Then Saynday got busy because he'd finished his
> thinking. He could begin to do things now.

'How far can you run?' he said to Fox.
'A long long way,' said Fox.
'How far can you run?' he said to Deer.
'A short long way,' said Deer.
'How far can you run?' he said to Magpie.
'A long short way,' said Magpie.
'I can't run very far myself,' said Saynday,
'So I guess I'll have to take it last.'
Then he lined them all out and told them what to
do.

In both cases the simplicity is rich and is helped by the
repetition of words which gives the story rhythm and a narrative quality. Simplicity in these examples is part of the
quality of writing and is effective in the context. However in
other books large words and sentences may be needed to
convey mood, scene or conversation. Unusual words may
create humour, impart information or indicate meaning in
the context.

6. *Perhaps the subject content is a means of categorizing a book as a children's book?*

But are there subjects which can *only* be put into story form
for children, or can only be offered to adults? The whole of
human knowledge and experience in any period of time and
any geographical place is open to coverage in story form and
in information book form. The books that are suitable for
children are those which look at an aspect in a way with
which a child, at his stage of knowledge and development,
can cope. Many of the great themes in story can give awareness, knowledge, and an understanding of things which in
real life might be overwhelming. To many children what is
real life for them is fantasy for others, depending upon their
personal circumstances. So it is the *perspective* which creates
a literature for children, the angle from which the theme is

viewed through the characters, via the author. Whether the theme involves world issues, morals, emotions, child or adult relationships, peaceful or violent events, realistic or imaginary settings, animals, humans or objects, the angle of vision is what causes a book to catch the interest of a child, the uniting of the mind of the writer with the mind of the child. When the writer re-captures the child-like vision, or as Rosemary Sutcliff describes herself, has a pocket of unlived childhood, or is in tune with contemporary childhood's needs and interests then the result is a book which enables the child to 'see' life and to acquire insight. This causes him not only to say 'That was a good book, have you any more?', but in many cases, to have the unspoken and subconscious satisfaction of adding to his stature mentally, emotionally and linguistically.

7. What is children's literature?
It is the written word which collectively embraces all the features mentioned so far, subject matter, characters and settings, style of writing and use of vocabulary presented from an angle of vision which matches the child's perspective. 'Good' literature is that which also increases his perception. But this body of literature is made up of thousands of individual books, each the product of someone's brain, each different from the other, providing for differing languages, differing interests, differing needs and differing levels of reading ability.

However good a book is and however marketed, promoted and recommended, we cannot say that *every* child must read the book, or *every* child will enjoy the book, for a child will not read voluntarily unless he enjoys the experience or needs the information, any more than adults will, voluntarily, spend time on books which do not engage their minds or their hearts.

The next chapter looks at the development of children's literature.

Further readings

Haviland, Virginia. ed. *Children's Literature; views and reviews*. London, Bodley Head, 1974

Kirkpatrick, D. L. *Twentieth Century Children's Writers*. London, Macmillan, 1978

Lewis, C. S. On three ways of writing for children. In S. Egoff et al. *Only Connect*. Toronto, O.U.P., 1969

Meek, M. ed. *The Cool Web; the pattern of children's reading*. London, Bodley Head, 1977

CHAPTER THREE

The Development of Children's Literature

Much modern children's literature has its roots in the past, in both form and content; many current attitudes towards children's books are based in the past and in much contemporary sub-literature, or popular literature, there are points of comparison with the 'penny dreadfuls' of earlier times.

That body of literature called the 'classics' is not a once-and-for-all list of great books but a growing body, being added to continually over the years as new books are written, read and acknowledged to be works that stand the test of time.

Time is of the essence in a study of the development of children's literature, in that literature often reflects the time, the relationship of the content of books to the social and cultural time; the technical sophistication of the time as it makes possible methods of book illustration and book production; the religious and educational influences at each period of time affecting literacy; the governmental and political influences of the time in the legislative control or promotion of books via publishing, bookselling and libraries.

The following brief outline of development is intended as background information. Those who are interested in the considerable amount of deeper detailed research into the history of children's literature will find recommendations for further reading at the end of the chapter.

It is a fact that much of what is known throughout the world as children's literature today has its origin in English history, in which a combination of circumstances contributed

30

to the condition under which a literature best develops.

Every country has its myths, legends and folk tales, passed on orally from generation to generation in times past and today, but the printing of such tales by Caxton in fifteenth-century England provided a basis for development and extension into later centuries. Puritanism had a didactic, moral and religious effect on books and education, exemplified in James Janeway's A *Token for Children*; an exact account of the conversion, holy and exemplary lives and joyful deaths of several young children. Similarly didactic was John Bunyan's *Pilgrim's Progress*, not written for children but adopted by them for the adventure story rather than the Christian allegory. John Locke, philosopher and educationist had a moral influence on the content of books for children and also sent fairy stories underground. Perrault in France had collected the courtly tales of Cinderella, Sleeping Beauty, Red Riding Hood, Puss-in-Boots and many others, and these were widely acclaimed across the Channel, but Locke's disapproval of fairy stories caused them to appear in chapbook form in England, which, as is the case with many things that are disapproved of or banned, gave them a wider market than might otherwise have happened.

Chapbooks, tiny 'paperbacks', were sold by chapmen or pedlars or travelling salesmen, to the same kind of mass market as the modern popular paperback books have today. Locke's disapproval was carried on into the eighteenth century by Mrs Trimmer and the Sunday School movement. Ironically the Sunday School movement, in its function of educating the working population, increased literacy and therefore readers, creating a religious literature to feed their needs, but many of the newly literate adults and young people found the popular literature more attractive.

Though there were many such adult books adopted by children for reading, and many educational reading books, the start of the specifically secular literature for children was provided by the printer and bookseller John Newbery (after whom the American children's literature award is named) in 1744. *The Little Pretty Pocket Book, History of Little Goody Two Shoes*, and *The Lilliputian Magazine* were all aimed at middle-class children and were a mixture of information, moral story and entertainment.

By the turn of the eighteenth century and throughout the nineteenth century there were changes in society which helped to develop children's literature, the greatest being in education. The Sunday School movement, the growth of the Mechanics Institutes for the education of the workers, and the start of education for all children created a more literate population. This in turn led to an increase in private and organization libraries and in 1850 to the first Public Libraries Act. Towards the end of the nineteenth century compulsory education for children, the invention of lithography, mechanical papermaking and cloth binding coincided to enable the standardized mass production of books, which meant the possibility of a greater quantity of any book and the consequent reduction in cost, the possibility of colour illustration and the wider attraction of books to a mass literate population.

Social barriers were breaking down and children were beginning to be seen as human beings in their own right, to be informed and educated but also to be entertained, and writers responded to this freedom by creating a body of literature which has come to be known as the golden age of children's literature, a period which continued up to the 1920s. A few examples of children's books from 1850 to 1932 will serve to justify this description, *Alice in Wonderland, Children of the New Forest, The Water Babies, Tom Brown's Schooldays, King of the Golden River, The Jungle Book, At the Back of the North Wind, Treasure Island, Lear's Book of Nonsense*, Beatrix Potter's books, *Wind in the Willows, Dr. Dolittle, Winnie the Pooh, Peter Pan, The*

Phoenix and the Carpet and *The Hobbit*.

These titles exemplify the diverse genres. From the largely didactic literature of the early years there developed the adventure story, fantasy, humour, humanized animals, the kind of imaginative literature which is the bonus for those children in every country who have mastered the mechanics of reading and achieved the degree of fluency necessary for the enjoyment of reading.

After the First World War when the social order had changed and international influences were felt, the 1920s and 1930s showed a growth in adventure and family stories with Arthur Ransome's *Swallows and Amazons* and Enid Blyton's *Famous Five* books, Richmal Crompton's *Just William* books and W. E. Johns' *Biggles*, which have maintained their popularity to the present day.

Also in the 1920s and 1930s that truly British institution, the boarding school, was the setting for the genre known as the school story, which achieved enormous popularity in many parts of the world both then and now. Such authors as Angela Brazil, Elsie Oxenham and Eleanor Brent-Dyer created schools in which mysteries, challenges and excitement provided wish fulfilment for many girls while authors such as Talbot Baines, Gunby Hadath and Frank Richards entertained the boys with tales of rivalry, adventure and fun in boys' boarding schools.

Most of the authors in this period serialized their stories in the numerous magazines of the time, such as *Magnet, Gem, Sunny Stories, Boys Own, Girls Own* and *Aunt Judy's Magazine*, thus reaching a wider readership than book purchasers and library users. For this was the heyday of children's periodicals, whether largely print, or largely picture strip, as in the comics like *Film Fun, Girls Crystal, Dandy, Beano* and *Mickey Mouse*.

In this period too, official acknowledgement that children's literature could be worthy was seen in the establishment of the Newbery Medal in the USA in 1922 and the Carnegie Medal in the UK in 1936, both awarded for an outstanding children's book in each year; and the Caldecott Medal from 1938 in the USA and the Greenaway Medal from 1955 in the UK for outstanding illustrated children's books in each year. For by this time some notable work was coming from illustrators in many countries, the result of developments in colour printing and of the widening market for children's books. Alongside the expansion of children's fictional reading material came the development of the non-fiction work for children, both individual information books and children's encyclopaedias. A period of recession followed, during the Second World War, after which came another flowering of talent and the development of different kinds of children's books. The works of William Mayne, Lucy M. Boston, Alan Garner, C. S. Lewis, Philippa Pearce, Rosemary Sutcliff, Henry Treece and many others include books praised as the 'new' classics, and were created from the 1940s on. Their work covered fantasy, historical novels and family stories producing a wealth of excellent literature.

Publishers by this time in the UK were proliferating to meet the demand of an increasingly large child population, the result of the birth rate expansion after the war. Television was not yet widely available and children needed books for leisure reading and books for school use because one of the results of the educational changes legislated by government was a move towards project/topic/child centred learning, which required a wide range and quality of information books.

By the 1960s a solid core of masterly writers was being acclaimed by the critics, librarians and by children. Children were also eagerly reading the work of popular writers and both child and parent were financially able to consider buying, which led in turn to the start of paperback publishing for children, initiated by the Penguin group in a series called

Puffins. From paperback story books to paperback picture books was a short step facilitated by the developments in printing processes, and the 1970s can be categorized as the time at which there was a coming together of certain conditions to produce not only a paperback readership but a new genre of books for young people, the teenage novel. Begun in the 1960s in the USA and developing there and in the UK and Sweden in the 1970s, the teenage novel was the result of the following conditions:

1. The postwar population bulge had then reached teenage.
2. The economic climate which provided well-paid employment for teenagers, possibly for the first time in history, meant that money was available to gratify their needs and desires, thus there was a market for specifically teenage literature.
3. There was the recognition by writers and publishers that here was a new breed of reader, too old for children's books, not yet emotionally mature enough for many adult books, with a definable set of interests, anxieties and problems.

The influence of television, world events, travel and wider education had opened up the world in all its aspects, creating a mood in which social realism became a major factor in books for children and young people. The number of series aimed at particular age or ability groups greatly increased both in fiction and information books. By the end of the 1970s the combination of educational need and effect, technical developments, social conditions and national and international influences, had produced in the UK and the USA a body of literature for children, ranging from toy books, picture books, cartoon/picture strip, to story books for various reading ages and abilities on almost every imaginable subject, and non-fiction covering most themes to varying depths for varying ages and abilities, all in varying degrees of quality.

This quantity of literature meant a greater choice for children, providing books for every need in a choice of popular, medium and highbrow, and often in a format of paperback or hardback.

Over the years the increasing range made necessary book selection by librarians, and guidance to children, teachers and parents on the suitability and use of books, the display and promotion of children's books, all requiring knowledge on the part of librarians. This led to the inclusion of children's literature in librarianship studies and to the creation of specialist posts in children's and school librarianship. It led also to the co-operation which now exists between writers, publishers, booksellers, librarians and teachers, and the child reader.

In any country the development of children's literature reflects that society's developments, not only in the literature's subject content but in style, format and availability.

The broad sociological effects are the result of religious, educational, psychological and political philosophies and practices. These also have an effect on the development of the book trade, on communication media and travel and on the social status of children. Another factor is the capacity of the language to express adequately in literary form in order to produce children's literature, while further influences upon development include not only the availability of libraries to provide the means of reading but the availability of alternative leisure pursuits which preclude the time or the need for reading.

Historically all these factors appear to have been present in England positively and constructively and beneficially, producing a body of children's literature which was read by children in many other countries, in English and in translation, until these countries had a literature of their own. Some countries must still rely on a 'borrowed' literature in that their conditions are not yet conducive to producing an indigenous literature. Not only were the English conditions ripe for producing the first golden age of children's literature and contributory to the second golden age, but they created also an established book trade which provided writers in other countries with the possibility of publication in Britain, where there was little or no possibility in their own country. That established children's book trade was developed from the early eighteenth century with about 6 books, to the early twentieth century with hundreds of books, to the present day with approximately 3,000 new children's book titles per year in Britain.

In many countries there is still a national children's literary history to be made. Developments are slow though knowledge, goodwill and talent exist and though international influence can be added to the list of factors that affect literary development.

The next chapter carries the concept of influential trends forward to the present day.

Further readings

Darton, F. J. Harvey. *Children's Books in England; five centuries of social life*. London, C.U.P., 1958

Ellis, Alec. *A History of Children's Reading and Literature*. London, Pergamon, 1968

Hurlimann, Bettina. *Three Centuries of Children's Books in Europe*. London, O.U.P., 1967

Meigs, Cornelia. *A Critical History of Children's Literature*. New York, Macmillan, 1970

Ray, Colin. *Background to Children's Books*. London, National Book League, 4th. ed. 1977

Ray, Sheila. *The Blyton Phenomenon*. London, Deutsch, 1982

Scott, Dorothea, H. *Chinese Popular Literature and the Child*. Chicago, ALA, 1980

Townsend, John Rowe. *Written for Children*. London, Kestrel, 1974

CHAPTER FOUR

The Children's Book Publishing Scene

The creation of a book for children follows a pattern of procedure common to most countries; author, publisher, bookseller, reviewer, reader. Many other people may be involved in the means of producing and distributing the book or information about the book, for example:

literary agents who, on behalf of the writer or illustrator are responsible for obtaining a publisher for a piece of work and for negotiating the best terms for that work
printers and binders
publicity and public relations personnel
reviewers and review media
critics and critical literature in the form of books and journal articles
associations and societies concerned with children and books
teachers and lecturers in children's literature
students of children's literature
librarians, libraries and special collections of children's books, both national and local
researchers and research organizations and collections concerned with the study of children's literature
radio, television and press people connected with book programmes and columns
commercial companies
educational institutions
individuals and their interests
children as readers

The children's book scene starts with the author or illustrator and some aspects of the work involved are shown in the next chapter. But the relationship between author and publisher can be indicated here.

Author and publisher

There are some specialist children's book publishers but publishing houses tend to have a children's list in addition to their general list and subject specialist lists. There are many publishers who do not include children's books at all, but even within the range of publishers of books for children there are some that specialize in certain kinds or series of children's book, so intending authors and illustrators need to be aware of the publisher's requirements.

In addition to commercial publishing houses there may be small printing companies who also publish, government publishing departments, specialist organizations and societies producing material for children, and individual people who publish privately. There are also countries where all books emanate from the state publishing house, for example China, USSR, Czechoslovakia, German Democratic Republic, Bulgaria and Hungary, while Tunisia gives some state support to children's book publishing.

Although publishers in many book-developed countries receive unsolicited manuscripts of both fiction and non-fiction from hopeful writers, few are accepted for publication. Often the reason is poor quality of writing, often that the theme has already been covered, and increasingly as costs rise, there is the obvious commercial factor of the need to ensure that the book will sell in sufficient quantity to cover costs or make a profit.

Generally children's books are commissioned from an outline or idea provided by the intending author or illustrator. This may have been offered unsolicited or invited on request from the children's book editor. Children's book editors, whether for fiction or information books, are constantly looking for original ideas and for possible gaps in the literature. When an idea or gap is seen the editor may approach an already published author or, in the case of non-fiction, a person who is knowledgeable in that field, and discuss the possibility of writing such a book.

Many already published authors and illustrators have a clause in their previous contract requiring them to offer their next book to the publisher. If author and publisher agree on the need, content and potential market for a book, the publisher draws up a contract which binds the author to delivering a manuscript of specified length by a specified date and binds the publisher to consider publication on specified financial terms, usually a percentage royalty basis, with special terms for paperback rights, foreign rights, film rights and book club fees, for example. If the terms are that the author is to receive ten per cent royalty payment on a published book price of £5.00, the breakdown of this price would be fifty pence to the author for each copy sold, the remaining £4.50 going to the publisher's production costs of printing, binding, distribution, publicity etc., the percentage given to the bookseller, and a percentage for publisher's profit.

The importance of sales promotion and marketing arrangements is therefore considerable if all concerned are to reap any financial benefit.

The children's book editor works closely with the author and illustrator during the writing/illustrating and when the finished work is submitted may send it to an outside 'reader' for an opinion. This may be a specialist in children's books or a specialist in the subject of the information book.

Co-production
In an effort to reduce costs some publishers make agreements with publishers in other countries. This happens mostly with

picture books where it is possible both for the colour plates to be printed in large quantities and for the photographic sheets to be available. In order to make a book suitable for a country other than the country of origin, a translated text or a new text can then be created and printed with the colour plates by the co-producing publisher. This kind of arrangement is common in Europe, the USA and Japan, but an example of co-publishing is the Asian Co-publication Programme administered by Unesco in Tokyo, where eight children's books have been written and published by the programme, each one in many different languages, through countries participating in the scheme.

There are disadvantages in co-production and co-publishing but greater availability of children's books and savings in production and publishing costs are distinct advantages.

Publisher and printer
Once the manuscript has been copy-edited for content and errors it will be marked up for the printer with instructions on typeface, layout, spacing etc. The graphic designer plans the total appearance and organizes the jacket design. In common with other books, children's books in many countries are given an international standard book number (ISBN) which identifies the publisher and the specific book. Orders for that book may be made by that number only, though for absolute accuracy it is wise to use author and title also as it is easy to make a mistake with writing or typing a number.

The typescript goes to the printer who may print the book by computer typesetting, photosetting, hot metal or other methods depending upon the printer, country and availability of technology. Galley proofs or sheets or proof copies will be sent to the editor to check for printers' errors and the editor and author will amend as necessary and return the proofs to the printer. The finished printing is then bound and sent to the distributors. From there copies are sent to reviewers, according to a pre-arranged list, to booksellers and other retailing outlets.

In those countries where there is a legal requirement a specified number of copies must be sent to the national library or its equivalent and this is known as legal deposit.

Advance publicity is made in the form of inclusions in the publisher's catalogue of forthcoming publications; notification to the book trade journals; leaflets and posters; mailing information to libraries, education authorities, overseas agents for the publisher; radio and television and the press; relevant organizations and individuals; and by other promotional activities.

From these, advance orders may be obtained, otherwise most of the sales in library-developed countries arise from purchase by libraries, organizations and individuals via library supply agencies, booksellers, stores and other bookselling outlets, or, in some countries, directly from the publishing house, the printer, the author or by other retailing methods.

The children's book as a finished product enters the children's book scene as a result of the work of author, illustrator, children's book editor, the design, financial, publicity and sales departments of the publishing house, the printer, binder and distributor.

Bookseller and purchaser

Booksellers and other retail outlets need to be persuaded to stock the book and their criteria are determined by the kind of buying public they serve, whether mass market, casual purchase, or specialists interested in and knowledgeable about children and books.

Examples of retail outlets include specialist children's bookshops, children's sections in general bookshops and large department stores, small selections in newsagents and neighbourhood shops, mobile bookshops and market stalls. In some countries library suppliers and large bookselling companies have showrooms in which the full range of children's fiction and non-fiction is on display and can be selected and purchased on the spot by librarians and others. In some cases these books are also processed by the supplier, using the purchasing library's labels, catalogue cards and classification number.

In the UK some public library systems include a purchase facility for school libraries as part of the schools library service. Some book suppliers offer 'approval' services whereby current publications each month are delivered to the library for the librarians to view and select according to need. Orders are made and the 'approval' boxes returned.

Book clubs and mail order sales of children's books are common in some countries, as is door-to-door selling in Japan. School bookshops are a powerful on-the-spot means of children making their own purchases. In the UK the School Bookshop Association is administered by a board of ten people representing publishers, bookshops and educationalists. The Association supports the work of about 6,000 bookshops in primary and secondary schools. These are staffed voluntarily by teachers or librarians in the school and open at times convenient for staff and students. Most are housed in semi-permanent or movable lockable shelf units and most are well used by the children.

Support services by the School Bookshop Association include a handbook, *How To Set Up and Run a School Bookshop*; children's book poster packs; a book bank card for saving towards a purchase; a do-it-yourself school bookshop plan for how to make a lockable unit to house books; badges, lists of books suitable for the initial opening of the bookshop, advice by mail and telephone, and the journal *Books For Keeps*. Some book suppliers and booksellers take part in the sale or return or other arrangement, involved in the local school's bookshop requirements.

Libraries form the major source of children's book purchase, but parents buying on behalf of their children, or accompanying their children, are to be seen in ordinary bookselling outlets.

Part of the children's book scene is occupied by the critics of children's books via the reviewing media, and by the literary analysis in literary journals and in books about children's books. Examples of these are given in the chapter on bibliographical aids.

The intending book purchaser may see the book in the bookshop or other selling outlet; or read a review in the review media or literary publication; or be introduced to it through a book club, for example, Israel's Clubs for the Encouragement of Reading, sponsored by the Ministry of Education; or through reading camps, as in Hungary's summer holiday camps designed to promote reading through a programme of talks, study, activities and reading.

If considering purchase on behalf of others, as for library stock, the selection criteria and clientele's needs and interests will be taken into account and, if appropriate, the book will be bought and eventually read, thus completing the chain of events from author to reader.

But the availability of children's books in any country is affected by a number of factors, some of which are discussed in the chapters on the development of, and trends in, children's literature.

Children's book publishing; the international scene
The publication of children's books depends upon government policies, political, economic and educational; the state of national literacy; the production and distribution outlets and communication media; the single language or multi-language conditions; the existence of libraries; the purchas-

ing power of institutions and individuals; and the freedom to read.

All of these must be taken into consideration when looking at statistics for children's book publishing. The following data is reproduced, with permission, from material published in 'International Year of the Child' as part of a Unesco discussion paper on *Children and Books*. The Table is taken from Part II of the paper – 'Some Statistical Data'. In this Table the major children's book-producing countries are seen to be, in order of highest number of titles published in the year, the UK, the USA, Federal Republic of Germany, the USSR, Japan and Korea. Some of the countries in the Table were represented at the Unesco Regional Workshop for Asian Writers and Editors of Books for Children and Juveniles. This was held in Seoul, Republic of Korea in 1978 and the report was published by the Unesco Regional Office for Culture and Book Development in Asia, in Pakistan in 1979.

Three areas were covered: the present provision of books and literacy, the kind of training available for writers and editors, and the countries' needs and problems regarding training.

In some of the Asian countries there was evidence of help from various sources. For example in Bangladesh the activities of Bangla Academy, the National Book Centre and National Children's Academy were contributing towards the growth of a children's literature. In Indonesia government aid was granted for the bulk purchase of books for libraries. In Korea the Korean Culture and Art Foundation had plans to produce 100 volumes of children's books based on the cultural tradition. India had three central government public trusts aiding publication, and the problem of the fourteen languages used in India.

Thailand's writing was strongly influenced by foreign popular stories and the Philippines imported 80% of its

Production of Children's Books: Number of Titles and Copies

Country	Year	Number of Titles	Number of copies (000)
AFRICA			
Egypt	1974	28	1070
Ghana	1976	4	—
Ivory Coast	1976	28	—
Kenya	1976	11	32
Libyan Arab Jamahiriya	1975	10	45
Malawi	1974	7	6
Mali	1975	2	6
Mauritania	1976	13	22
Nigeria	1975	72	521
Senegal	1976	6	60
South Africa	1974	333	1673
Sudan	1976	3	16
Tunisia	1976	18	250
United Rep. of Tanzania	1976	15	—
AMERICA, NORTH			
Canada	1976	142	—
Cuba	1976	54	4725
Mexico	1976	15	—
Panama	1975	2	1
United States of America	1976	2210	—
AMERICA, SOUTH			
Bolivia	1974	5	13
Brazil	1975	381	4111
Chile	1976	3	45
Colombia	1975	16	40
Guyana	1976	1	3
Peru	1976	3	—
Uruguay	1975	7	—

Production of Children's Books: Number of Titles and Copies

Country	Year	Number of Titles	Number of copies (000)
ASIA			
Bangladesh	1974	2	5
Brunei	1975	5	34
Burma	1974	95	753
Cyprus	1976	14	35
Hong Kong	1976	48	139
India	1976	448	—
Indonesia	1976	188	—
Israel	1975	113	1237
Japan	1976	1892	—
Jordan	1976	47	832
Korea, Republic of	1976	1158	2207
Malaysia	1976	193	664
Maldives	1976	5	—
Philippines	1976	42	25
Singapore	1976	29	158
Syrian Arab Republic	1976	6	19
Thailand	1976	15	—
Vietnam, Socialist Rep. of	1975	54	2349
EUROPE			
Austria	1976	147	—
Bulgaria	1976	149	6805
Czechoslovakia	1976	297	9166
Finland	1976	161	—
France	1974	604	—
German Democratic Rep.	1976	432	10001
Germany, Federal Rep. of	1976	2056	—
Greece	1976	144	—
Hungary	1976	81	3400
Iceland	1976	47	—

Production of Children's Books: Number of Titles and Copies

Country	Year	Number of Titles	Number of copies (000)
Ireland	1976	1	—
Italy	1976	434	9695
Luxembourg	1976	2	—
Malta	1976	10	—
Norway	1976	217	—
Poland	1976	230	9212
Romania	1976	134	4640
Spain	1976	825	8506
United Kingdom	1976	2269	—
Yugoslavia	1976	301	2359
OCEANIA			
Australia	1976	53	—
New Zealand	1976	11	—
Tonga	1976	1	10
Western Samoa	1976	5	2
U.S.S.R. (including Byelorussian S.S.R. and Ukranian S.S.R.)	1976	2025	159450

Taken from: *Part II – Some Statistical Data.*
Unesco; Division for Book Promotion and Encouragement of International Cultural Exchanges. *I.Y.C. Discussion Paper on Children and Books.* New York, I.Y.C. Secretariat, 1979.

children's books in the English language. Here there was a long-term programme for producing children's books, developed by the Children's Literature Association in the Philippines Inc. (CLAPI).

Nepal was concentrating on textbooks and had geographical and literacy problems in addition to the problem of a small population.

Overall the problems referred to in the Report centred on the shortage of printing materials, the system of payment to authors and bulk purchasing by institutions. The need for training for writers and editors was seen to encompass writing, illustrating, production, distribution, research and evaluation; the impact of book reading on children, the relevance of cultural and literary values, and age and sex relevance. After these, further training was thought to include psychology, communication, techniques of writing/printing/ editing/technology; reading, analysis of language, and the economics of publishing.

In terms of the content of children's books, the need was seen as folk tales, heroic tales, tales from local and neighbouring countries with similar culture, and local contemporary stories.

The children's book people of many countries meet at least annually at one or other of the big book fairs. The Bologna Book Fair in Italy attracts about 800 children's book publishers from over 50 countries, who display their publications and their forthcoming publications, and some of their authors and illustrators. Here there is the opportunity not only to see the world's output of new children's books, but also to bid for the foreign rights or to arrange co-production.

Similarly at the annual Frankfurt Book Fair in Germany, publishers attempt to promote their books although this Fair includes the whole range of each publisher's output, for adult or child.

The Bratislava Fair in Czechoslovakia is concerned with book illustrations, while the Jerusalem Book Fair in Israel includes children's books in general. The Unicef Collection in New York, USA provides a sample of children's books from many countries.

Several children's literature meetings take place each year, attended by interested people from all parts of the world. Examples include IBBY (International Board on Books For Young People) which has a conference on a children's book theme each year. The Loughborough Conference on Children's Literature meets in a different country each year on an ad hoc basis, the only administrative address being that of the host country's organizers. The International Association for Research in Children's and Youth Literature promotes research into literature and reading for young people and meets for members' discussions.

Individual countries hold seminars which are open to all, and at all such international events, publishers, authors, illustrators, graphic designers, librarians, critics and interested individuals can meet to talk about children's books, to negotiate production and promotion arrangements, and to see the ways in which children's books are developing, for the scenery changes in the children's book world.

Further readings

Barto, Agnia. The training of specialists for the production of books for children in Russia. *Bookbird*, no. 1. 1975 pp. 10–66

Bookbird. All issues.

British Printing Industries Federation/Publishers Association. *Putting the Book in Hand, Including Preparation up to Composition*. London, BPIF, 1975

Pellowski, A. *Made to Measure; children's books in developing countries*. Paris, Unesco, 1980

Turow, J. *Getting Books to Children; publisher-market relations*. Chicago, ALA, 1978

Unesco. *Children and Books*. IYC Discussion Paper. Paris, Unesco, 1979

CHAPTER FIVE

Children's Books – Fiction and Non-fiction

In most countries there are books for children, whether the literature is indigenous or imported, in the vernacular, the national language or another language. These books tend to follow a pattern of theme and structure whatever the country, so this chapter looks at some of those themes and forms, their development and nature and the relationship to children.

Although many of the examples cited are books in the English language, comments made are applicable to books in any language. The information given is intended to enable the interested reader to see some of the aspects common to children's books; to perceive the connection between the examples given and other books in the same genre; to note the aspects found in children's books in most countries or languages, and to follow up the subject by further reading of the critical works about each genre.

The most important preparation and continuation, however, is to read the actual children's books available. Reading for possible library selection, for reviewing, for class use or for storytelling, is one kind of reading but the children's book person who wants to be truly familiar with children's books must read throughout the range as a matter of both professional and personal interest.

The aspects discussed in this chapter are:

Myths, legends, folk and fairy tales
Fantasy
Animal stories
Historical stories
Humour, comics and picture strips

School stories
Adventures stories
Family stories
Realism
Books for teenagers
Poetry
Information books

Myth, legend, folk and fairy
There are numerous different versions in the forms of anthologies, collected editions, one-story picture books, illustrated and non-illustrated versions, simplified, translated, or censored.

In most countries there are variations too on themes; the creation theme, variants on Cinderella, the frog prince, the trickster, the magic object to be touched, the dragon, the small but brave man, the use of the number three as in three wishes, three little pigs. In most countries the traditional tales are passed on orally; in some countries, also in print, and in some additionally by means of drama and film.

Any re-telling of an old myth, legend, folk or fairytale must retain the characteristics of the original if it is to increase the knowledge and insight of the reader or the hearer. But because these stories are essentially oral tales they become different once they are written down, so the best are those which manage to retain the narrative quality in a vigorous colloquial style with the pattern of speech. The best too are also able to reflect the depth of psychological or emotional content which has enabled them to be as relevant to human nature today as they were to previous generations right back to the beginnings of the human race.

Often the illustration of such tales spoils the mental picture which the good textual versions can create in the reader's or hearer's mind, so the best illustrated editions of such tales are those in which the pictures truly illustrate the essence of the text. There are scholarly and classic versions, popular and shallow versions, and writers and publishers are constantly trying to find a suitable way of transmitting the stories that Plato called the highest and most natural form of education for young children.

Myths and legends
The myths are about gods, the origins of evil, of the world, of man's struggle against strange and strong elements and his own human nature. If they are considered as springing from primitive man's emotions and as attempted explanations for the world's existence and man's place in it in story form, we can trace the continuity of elemental emotions, instincts and human nature. This can throw light on our attitudes and beliefs today, which are often difficult to see under layers of sophisticated and civilized protection.

As Alan Garner has said, 'distilled and violent truths' are the basic ingredients of most of the myths. They are truths appealing to contemporary minds as much as to those of other generations and have a thread running through them all of something outside ourselves, or above us, controlling human beings and life, something supernatural, often using men like playthings. These gods achieved their ends by violent means either physical, in tearing up mountains, creating floods, or by intimidation as in the Jason story, or by testing or punishment as with Atlas and Sysiphus, or by violent emotions such as lust, desire, anger, jealousy, fear and love.

Many re-tellings have softened the potential power by omitting the too violent or too adult emotional parts, or by re-phrasing to suggest something less excessive, so many versions are dull because their excitement has gone and left a boring tale about people with unpronounceable names. Illustrations too have toned down the emotions and depict mainly events.

Illustrator Charles Keeping, who believes that the myths

are all about human feelings, found that although *God Beneath the Sea* by Leon Garfield and Edward Blishen, was a long book, and the authors could express everything in many words, he had only fifteen drawings through which to give visual expression. He therefore turned from costume or plot depiction, which could date or simply duplicate the words, and attempted to convey emotions in the stories. He had such success that many adults were shocked by the force of his black and white drawings.

Legends and folk tales

As with myths the origins of legends lie in the oral tradition of storytelling about supposed happenings and the actions and exploits of individuals. Just as we may tell a friend about something someone has done, in our own words, so the story got its second and third telling and then was passed on by others who added bits they had heard or used their imaginations to liven up aspects to entertain their listeners. We take legends not as faithfully reported happenings but as stories woven around a character or event.

The legends and folk tales are often attempts over the years to give some explanation, as in the North American legend of *How Saynday Got the Sun*, or the Papua New Guinea tribal tales of primordial events. Other legends are concerned with heroes, heroines and villains, whether human or animal. In Britain there are King Arthur and Robin Hood; in Scandinavia Balder and Beowulf, and Grettir, Mastermaid; in France Roland; in the USA Pecos Bill and Johnny Appleseed and Brer Rabbit; in parts of Africa and the West Indies there is Anansi the Spiderman; in China there is Monkey; in Ireland Finn McCool, and in Australia Bunyip.

Research shows that tales which initially seem to be exclusive to one area or tribe, often have strong similarities to those of quite different areas or countries. It can be suggested that most legends and folk and fairy tales are founded on one or more of the following basic aspects:

Weakness and strength
Bravery and cowardice
Poverty and riches
Cleverness and stupidity
Quest and achievement
Potential coming to fruition
Heroes and villains
Triumph of good over evil.

These are exemplified in such collections of stories as Virginia Haviland's *Faber Book of North American Legends*, Helen Mitchnik's *Egyptian and Sudanese Folk Tales*, James Riordan's *Tales from Central Russia*, Grace Hallworth's *Listen to the Story: tales from the West Indies*, Carola Oman's *Robin Hood*, and Barbara Leonie Picard's *Hero Tales from the British Isles*, William McAlpine's *Japanese Tales and Legends*, J. E. B. Gray's *Indian Tales and Legends*, and Kevin Crossley-Holland's *Book of Northern Legends*.

Fairy stories
Though some fairy stories are about fairies, elves and pixies, the majority are not, but are concerned with people who are apparently human beings, who find themselves in situations where magic transforms, aids or confounds them. Fairyland can be defined as a world in which enchanted and enchanting things happen, a world which has a place also in the inner mind.

A great deal has been written about fairy stories, describing and analysing, looking for psychological significance, geographical similarity, historical background, imaginative effect on children's minds, and ways of telling, presenting and illustrating fairy stories. A selection of readings covering

55

these aspects is given at the end of the chapter.

Most countries have their fairy stories and in most countries the characters are not usually children, though illustrators often depict them as such. Characters in fairy stories tend to be adult, such as Cinderella, Sleeping Beauty and Bluebeard from Perrault's tales; Rapunzel, Snow White and the Dancing Princesses from Grimm's tales; or Andersen's Princess (and the Pea), Tin Soldier, and the Emperor who thought he had new clothes; or Sinbad the Sailor from the *Arabian Nights' Entertainments*. Sometimes the characters are animal as in *The Ugly Duckling* or indefinable as in Tolkien's Hobbit.

So the appeal to children is not identification with the age of the character but with the style and structure of the story and with its inner truth, which in many cases has persisted for a very long time. Western fairy tales are considered to derive from just a few sources. These include:

1. Seventeenth-century *1001 Nights* or the *Arabian Nights' Entertainments* which were culled from a sixth-century Arabian manuscript of stories told in the middle-eastern palaces.
2. Giambattista Basile, the court writer to the Italian princes in the seventeenth century, who is thought to have invented Cinderella and Sleeping Beauty and a number of stories of horror and murder.
3. Charles Perrault who in the seventeenth century collected stories for telling at the French court, many of which had to be considerably expurgated for later readers.
4. The Grimm Brothers, Jakob and Wilhelm, whose first collection of stories in 1812 arose from their work as philologists.
5. Hans Christian Andersen of Denmark whose stories were translated into English in 1846.

6. Joseph Jacobs of England, who collected English fairy tales from books rather than oral tradition, with examples like *Jack and the Beanstalk, Dick Whittington* and *The Three Bears*.
7. Andrew Lang in the 1890s who edited many volumes of collected fairy stories, such as *The Blue Fairy Book* and *The Yellow Fairy Book*.

Whatever their origin, and many versions and identical themes appear in many countries' tales, they all contain those aspects I listed under legends and folk tales, and they all have either a happy ending or one in which just retribution is seen. The best tellings or re-tellings, also use narrative flow, from the oral origins, a flow which is perpetuated today by oral telling at mother's knee or in storytelling sessions, in the spoken dialogue in films and televised versions, and, in Britain particularly, in the Christmas pantomimes based on fairy tales.

The structure of the storyline, the vivid description, the economy of words, the clear and simple character studies, are part of the need to get the story across to a listener. The inner truth that retains his interest and leaves him satisfied is demonstrated in the underlying 'moral' in most of the tales: pride in *The Red Shoes* and in *The Emperor's New Clothes*; greed in *Pinocchio, Big Claus and Little Claus* and *The Golden Goose*; self esteem in *The Ugly Duckling*; values of life and death in *The Emperor's Nightingale*; bravery in *The Little Tailor* and *Hansel and Gretel*.

There are thousands of published books of fairy tales throughout the world, some in collected editions but increasingly, as colour printing and picture book production improve, there are picture book re-tellings of an individual story. In some picture fairy story books there is a discrepancy between the theme and the feeling of the story as told in words, and what should be a complementary style of illustration. I have already mentioned Charles Keeping's powerful illustrations complementing the strongly worded text of a book of myths, but there is in print a story of Cinderella that is told in earthy modern-style language but illustrated in pale silvery, romanticized style. Such lack of sympathy does not enhance the whole effect of the book, nor aid the child reader.

However, the spirit of the fairy tale is magnificently captured in individual ways by artists and book illustrators such as Jri Trnka of Czechoslovakia, Ib Spang Olsen of Denmark, Lilo Fromm and Janosch of Germany, Monika Laimgrüber of Switzerland, Maurice Sendak of the USA and Errol Le Cain of Britain.

Many fairy stories contain quite horrific events, such as cutting off feet and shoes in *The Red Shoes*, a dead grandmother's body being used to trick someone in *Big Claus and Little Claus*, a child-eating ogre in *Mollie Whuppy*, and Bluebeard's murders of his womenfolk. As in re-tellings of the myths and legends, some versions tone down the violence or omit the more bloodthirsty aspects. But most tales have a high standard of behaviour and principle and most children safely enjoy the more fearful aspects.

The traditional fairy tale, world wide, allows the reader or the listener to see or hear that time and place are of no concern. The traditional start to the story 'Once upon a time' is both a stimulator and a pacifier. The fairy story allows the child or adult to follow a clear progression of action and dialogue with no doubt as to who is the good character and who the bad, and with the satisfaction of seeing the former triumph over difficulty with or without magical aid, and the latter getting his just deserts. But the fairy story has not ended with those considered to be traditional. Modern fairy stories exist including Jay Williams' *The Practical Princess and Other Liberating Fairy Tales*. The same ingredients are found in the modern stories as in the old fairy stories and all are set in the same enchanted land.

But the child who has loved fairy stories from babyhood may find interest waning around the age of nine, boys sooner than girls. At that age there is often a transition to a stronger liking for what is termed fantasy.

Fantasy

Fantasy is not confined to books. Children and adults fantasize all the time over matters in their own, and other's lives. They fantasize about their toys or possessions, their relationships, their past and their future lives. Fantasy is an integral part of the thought process. So when Margery Fisher says in *Intent Upon Reading*, 'Fantasy takes known objects and scenes and re-shapes them in its own terms', she is speaking not only about books but about a human condition. She says, 'We may properly call those stories fantasy which bring the magic and irrational into our own world'.

We can make a number of inferences from that. For example there is the inference that magic from another world enters our 'real' world as in Helen Cresswell's *The Nightwatchmen* or E. M. Nesbit's *Five Children and It*. There is the inference that parts of our world, to which we do not normally go, have magic areas, such as the under-sea world in Lucy M. Boston's *The Sea-Egg*, Charles Kingsley's *The Water Babies* or Jules Verne's *20,000 Leagues under the Sea*. We can go to our world in the past via a magic clock in *Tom's Midnight Garden* by Philippa Pearce. We can see a complete world under the floor in Mary Norton's *The Borrowers*, or under the earth in Raymond Briggs' *Fungus the Bogeyman* and Elizabeth Beresford's *The Wombles*. Or we can be immersed in the fantasy world of Never-Never Land in J. M. Barrie's *Peter Pan* or in *Alice in Wonderland*. Tove Jansson offers a humorous saga of creatures in *Moominland* while Norton Juster takes a child reader to Dictionopolis and Digitopolis in *The Phantom Tollbooth*.

We can travel to mythical worlds created by J. R. R. Tolkien in *The Hobbit* and *The Lord of the Rings*; to the land of Prydain created by Lloyd Alexander in his five-book cycle; to the fantasy places of Alan Garner's *Owl Service*; to the land of *Narnia* with C. S. Lewis in his series, examplified in *The Lion, the Witch and the Wardrobe*; Ursula le Guin's *A Wizard of Earthsea* and Susan Cooper's books create fantasy worlds brilliantly.

Fantasy can also be seen in the stories of animals and toys who take on human attributes, whether a teddy bear called *Winnie the Pooh*, the woodland life in *Wind in the Willows*, or in the pilgrimage of toys in *The Mouse and His Child*, by Russell Hoban. Similarly Robert C. O'Brien's *Mrs. Frisby and the Rats of Nimh* holds up a picture of the 'real' world through the story of rats building a new and better society. Perhaps the best animal fantasy of recent times is E. B. White's *Charlotte's Web* in which spider and pig collaborate.

The fantasy of monsters is seen in Maurice Sendak's *Where the Wild Things Are* and in Ted Hughes' *The Iron Man*, both of which use an economy of words yet offer an immense richness of imagery and suspense.

The future world is a world of fantasy in that in science fiction known objects and present happenings are built on, to project an imaginary world of the future as rooted in reality as those stories which take a mythical setting for the base. Thus the books by John Christopher, Robert Heinlein, Alan Nourse and Monica Hughes present, along with those of Ray Bradbury, H. G. Wells and Isaac Asimov, a picture of *this* world by the emphases they lay on aspects of another world or our world in the future. Nicholas Fisk, Peter Dickinson and Madeleine L'Engle imagine life in the future in some of their books, fantasies making use of a thought-through interpretation of where today's trends will lead us tomorrow.

Animal stories

A large proportion of children's books are concerned with animals, birds or insects of one kind or another, possibly on the grounds that they are ageless and timeless. They can be given attributes and faults not acceptable in child characters. They are known to provide the psychological comfort that children find in pets.

Animal stories vary from fantasy humanized animals to the simply informative about animal life. Animals behaving like humans are often a vehicle for a message and some of the earliest stories such as *Aesop's Fables* used animals to point a moral, and many of the folk tales have animal heroes or anti-heroes, such as Anansi and Monkey.

Books for older readers have humanized animals too, such as the rabbits in *Watership Down* by Richard Adams, the rats of Nimh, or that classic of the twentieth century, *Animal Farm* by George Orwell. At all levels the animals usually behave as equivalent adult humans would or should, so humanized adult animals are acceptable to the child reader where characters shown as adult humans are not. Examples include Beatrix Potter's *Mrs. Tiggywinkle,* the characters in *Wind in the Willows*, the spider and the pig in *Charlotte's Web, Frog and Toad* by Arnold Lobel and the church mice in Graham Oakley's series of stories.

Stories in which a child forms an affection for an animal are popular with many age groups and are found to be therapeutic for many. Perhaps the vicarious satisfying of a wish for a pet is the reason, providing also a means of having someone or something dependent. Examples include *A Dog So Small* by Philippa Pearce, a classic in its appeal and quality, in which a small boy longs for a dog. Throughout most of the book he talks and walks with his invented, tiny, imaginary dog and although there is a real dog at the end the reader is satisfied even with the dog so small. In Barry Hines' *Kestrel for a Knave*, David a young teenager has an unhappy home and school life, and rears a kestrel (a kind of hawk) lavishing time and love on it. In Jane Rees' *Horse of Air*, a teenage English girl finds solace in a Welsh pony who helps her through the break-up of her parents' marriage and her move to another town and another school. John Steinbeck's *Red Pony* has a similar theme.

Humorous stories about animals are numerous and the young reader of picture books has a wealth to choose from including Mary Rayner's *Mr and Mrs Pig's Evening Out*, Gene Zion's *Harry the Dirty Dog*, Elfrida Vipont's *Elephant and the Bad Baby* and Rudyard Kipling's *Just So Stories*.

Stories of real animals often become classics and are read by both adults and children, as these examples show; Henry Williamson's *Tarka the Otter*, Sheila Burnford's *The Incredible Journey*, undertaken by two dogs and a cat in their successful attempt to go four hundred miles back to their Canadian home; Paul Gallico's *Snow Goose*. Real animals are also used in the many photo-stories now available, such as Helen Piers' *Rabbit is Hungry*.

Popular with many girls, particularly in Britain, the USA and Australia, are the 'pony books'. There are large quantities in hardback and paperback and most are the work of a few prolific writers. The early classics *Black Beauty* by A. Sewell, *The Yearling* by M. Rawlings and Enid Bagnold's *National Velvet*, were forerunners of pony books written in recent years at a popular level for the 'horse-mad' girls of twelve upwards. Each of the following writers has written many pony books: Mary Treadgold, Ruby Ferguson, Christine and Diana Pullein-Thompson, Primrose Cumming, Judith M. Berrisford, Monica Edwards; while other writers such as Vian Smith and K. M. Peyton created novels around the theme of ponies.

The books are avidly read by some girls who may or may not possess a pony, but the interest tends to wane when late teenage provides other interests.

However, it is clear that animal stories, of whatever kind, fill a need in the child reader for something dependent upon him in a life where he is dependent upon adults; a need for the bravery of the hero animals and for the wider horizons that are made possible for him through humanized animals.

Historical stories

Most historical stories are read by the middle-to-older part of the children/young person age range and it is probable that three factors are the cause. The first is that many children need to be of an age to understand the present before they can appreciate the past. The second factor is that most historical writers for children use the kind of detail, descriptive writing and sentence patterns that demand good reading ability. The third factor lies in the age of the main character in the novel. This is usually between twelve and adulthood and the emphasis is often on the adult characters surrounding the child character, thus making the book more attractive to readers within that range than to younger children.

The historical story is in many forms. It can be history in story form, set around an actual historical character or event; it can be an adventure story in historical setting, either pure imagination or a mixture of fact and fiction; it can be time-slip from present to past (and back) or from past to present (and back).

Whichever of these forms the novel takes, the writer has undoubtedly done much research into the events, social customs, costume, practices and principles of the period or country, and any period or country is likely to be used by an author if it contains the elements of adventure and human interest necessary for an historical story. For instance some of Rosemary Sutcliff's books are set in Roman Britain, Leon Garfield's in eighteenth-century England. Jill Paton Walsh set *The Emperor's Winding Sheet* in Byzantine times and Mollie Hunter's *The Stronghold* is a story of the early Scottish defence against Scandinavian invaders in the first century.

Laura Ingalls Wilder's books act out the early American settlers' activities while Harold Keith's *Rifles for Watie* depicts life in the American Civil War. Elizabeth George Speare's *The Bronze Bow* is set in Israel in the time of Jesus.

Some of the books selected for the IBBY Honours List in 1980 were historical stories. Spain's book, by Joseph Vallverdu, entitled *Mir the Squirrel* involves a boy, Mir, in eleventh-century Catalonia, in the warfare of the Moorish invasion; Austria's book *Nataiyu's Long Journey* by Kathe Recheis, is the story of a young Blackfoot Indian in 1884. The German Juvenile Book Award for 1980 went to an anti-fascist historical novel by Ursula Fuchs called *Emma or the Restless Times*, set in the Second World War, over 40 years ago. One of the Netherlands' 'Best' books in 1979 was Thea Beckman's *Town in a Storm*, about the seventeenth-century occupation of Utrecht by the French.

The fact that the majority of historical works for children are based on war or conflict reflects one of the reasons given by many historical writers for choosing the past rather than the present time. The past offers a range of situations in which a child was pitted against misfortune or an enemy and could show bravery, cunning, achievements, loyalty and even love. Many authors feel better able to portray the social history of the past correctly than to understand and correctly define the present, so the two aspects of subject content and author inclination combine to produce the genre known as the historical novel for children.

Analysis shows that most authors give a clue to the period in the first page either by actually giving the date or indicating it by the use of an historical place or a name. Rosemary Sutcliff's *The Light Beyond the Forest* begins

> On every side, Camelot climbed, roof above coloured roof, up the steep slopes of the hill. About

the foot of the hill the river cast its shining silver
noose; and at the highest heart of the town rose the
palace of King Arthur.

This also exemplifies the style of writing which shows the
flavour of the period by the sentence structure and judicious
use of vocabulary rather than by imposing the idiom of the
period on to a modern style of writing. It also typifies the
kind of historical writing which is firmly in the period where
the characters think and act within the limits of their era
rather than a present view of past history where the characters are set in a past age but think like a modern character.
Such books also have something to say to the adult reader.

The responsibility of the illustrator of the historical story
is heavy. He must accurately portray the factual aspects of
the period while adding the flavour. It is common to find
black and white line drawings in the few illustrations to be
found in historical books for older readers. Picture story
books on an historical theme are rare and tend to be very
simple in text and flamboyantly colourful in illustration.

Although many kinds of book and reading interest are
common to many countries, the historical novel tends to be
found largely in Western countries with a long history of
children's book writing, and the books themselves tend to
appeal to a small but dedicated percentage of the child reading population.

Humour

Whether for adults or children humour in books takes many
forms and produces a variety of responses, from loud laugh-
ter to an inner feeling of emotional or intellectual amusement.

The most obviously funny forms of literature are the joke
books such as *The Old Joke Book* by Janet and Allan Ahlberg (most of whose other books have a strong humorous
content in both text and picture), and *Jokes and Fun* by

Helen Hoke. Then there are many anthologies of humour usually culled from the work of well-known writers. These can be either on a special theme, such as *A Dog's Life*; *A Canine Anthology*, selected by William Cole and including Benchley and Thurber stories, or general like Peter Dickinson's collection, *Presto! Humorous Bits and Pieces*.

The nonsense of Edward Lear and Norman Hunter, can also be linked with the books of humorous verse which often include the poems of writers such as Lewis Carroll, Spike Milligan, Ogden Nash and T. S. Eliot.

Situation comedy abounds in children's books such as Dorothy Edwards' *My Naughty Little Sister*, Astrid Lindgren's *Pippi Longstocking*, Richmal Crompton's *Just William*, Mary Rodgers' *Freaky Friday* and Florence Parry Heide's *The Shrinking of Treehorn*. Substitute children in the form of animals also provide fun as in Michael Bond's *Paddington* books, A. A. Milne's *Winnie the Pooh*, and John Burningham's *Mr Gumpy's Outing*.

For young people there is a range of books which can be read at both the serious and the comic levels, such as Paul Zindel's *The Pigman* and Betsy Byars' *The Eighteenth Emergency*, both examples of the art of providing an underlying comic vein in a serious theme, tragi-comedy, and both by American authors, who seem to be more adept at this than writers in other countries.

The illustrative content of children's books can also convey humour and there are many picture books in which the subject theme and the pictorial interpretation combine to create a 'funny' book. Examples include the Dr Seuss books; the work of the Ahlberg partnership as in *Burglar Bill*; the *Mrs. Pepperpot* books by Alf Prøysen, illustrated by Bjorn Berg; and anything by Quentin Blake.

But humour in books may not be appreciated by children in all countries. Not all humour is cross-national or translatable. The most common elements are associated with absurdities, surprise, incongruous situations, exaggeration, slap-stick and predicaments, whereas taboo, particularly lavatorial subjects and verbal humour are often peculiar to one country. Humour tends to parallel a child's emotional and verbal development in that it is necessary to know normality before being able to identify abnormality, to have some knowledge of language before being able to appreciate a play on words, puns or verbal humour. Some experience of life and its situations is necessary in order to understand when people and their institutions are being parodied or mocked in story or picture.

So humour in children's books tends to start with the young child's experience of doing, or not being allowed to do, 'naughty' things, and develops towards the adult subtle aspects of irony and satire.

Comics and picture strip books
The pictorial humour in comic books is very popular throughout the world and the quantity of such material increases both at the most commercial level and at the highest level as an art form.

Comics are usually attractive to look at, easy to read, and on themes similar to those found in books; family life, school, adventure, humour, sport, science fiction, war, romance.

Told in a sequence of narrative pictures, with succinct captions or 'balloon' talk, they capture the interest of a large proportion of children and young people. The immense popularity of picture strip for both children and adults lies in the following aspects:

1. The pictures, which tend to be informal, fluid, attracting the attention even in black and white; informative in indicating the next step in the visual story progression.

2. The contents, which basically conform to the contents of book plots in the elemental themes of love, hate, greed, pride, bravery, cowardice, good and evil, but all starkly simplified by the constraints of the picture strip format.
3. The familiarity of the regular characters and the familiarity of the formula that enables good to triumph over evil, the hero to win in the end and the moral to be made that goodness pays.
4. The regularity of the format and its weekly or monthly availability, which provides something to look forward to.
5. Comics being the least middle class of all reading matter for children, cut across social boundaries in both content and readership.
6. The inclusion of other features such as puzzles, questions, information snippets and things to do, give a magazine flavour.

Comics are easy to read and never boring, largely because several technical features aid the ease of reading and of comprehension. The frame surrounding each picture and the balloon surrounding much of the text, enable the eye, the mind and the attention to be concentrated in the required place. Some comics have picture strips which are informative in that they can be followed without the text, others can be found where the text can stand alone without the pictures; but taking the pictures, words and frames together, there is a powerful concentration of aids to comprehension.

Similarly the length of attention needed is short enough to ensure that it is achieved, length being one of the aspects that children mention in relation to their dislike of book reading.

Some comic strips cause concern in their stereotyped characters and racialist/nationalist/sexist prejudices, but the 'funnies' stereotyping can be taken less seriously in that it usually represents the safety valve for the relief of tension by mocking parents, teachers, librarians, bullies and authority. That children's lives are such that they enjoy this form of escapism, is a problem too large to discuss here but the fact is that children do find tilting at authority a source of amusement and do feel that justice has been done when all is restored to normal at the end. 'Funnies' head the poll in all published and most unpublished surveys of comic book reading.

As comics almost always form part of a larger reading diet or are read by those who are not capable of sustained book reading, the enjoyment of comics need not be denied children.

The picture strip of quality as an art form is seen in books such as Herge's *Tintin* series, the Goscinny and Uderzo *Asterix* books, and Raymond Briggs' *Father Christmas* and *Fungus the Bogeyman* books. Each of these has both textual and pictorial style and wit, requiring much more of the reader than the commercial comic strip, and offering, instead of surface pleasure, a depth of satisfaction.

School stories

The boarding or residential school is a particularly British tradition, though many other countries have them. Such a school lends itself to story form because it contains the seeds of adventure, the possibilities of strong and weak characters, authority in the shape of teachers but freedom in the absence of parents; all within the clearly defined framework of a school organization.

The surprising aspect of school stories is that though the majority were written in the period 1900 to 1960 they are not only still popular in the 1980s in Britain but have a wide readership in other countries, particularly in Malaysia and the Pacific areas.

The now less popular boys' school stories range from the documentary/adventure style of Thomas Hughes' *Tom Brown's Schooldays* and Talbot Baines' *Fifth Form at St. Dominic's*, to the lighthearted series of Frank Richard's *Billy Bunter* books and Anthony Buckeridge's *Jennings* books. The more modern school stories include those set in day schools rather than boarding schools, such as E. W. Hilditch's *Jim Starling* books and William Mayne's choir school books. A controversial novel *The Chocolate War*, by Robert Cormier, swings the balance right over to present day realism in its depiction of a corrupt American school teacher, an extortion racket, and one boy's attempts to break the vicious circle.

Girls' school stories are vast in quantity, ranging from the archetypal Angela Brazil books to the fifty-six titles in the *Chalet School* series by Elinor Brent-Dyer, and the numerous titles in the *Abbey School* series by Elsie Oxenham. Enid Blyton's school stories were popular from their beginning in the 1940s and remain so today in three series, *The Naughtiest Girl*, the *St Clare's* and the *Malory Towers* books.

Nearer the present day Mary Harris's *The Bus Girls* exemplifies the school story set in a more realistic world. But the essence of the appeal of the earlier books lies in the dream fulfilment of being liked, achieving success in sport, hero-worshipping the sixth-former or the teacher, or solving a mystery connected with the school or the family.

Many of the plots are repetitive, the characters stereotyped, the slang outdated; there is little to do with real-life boarding school practice in the educational sense and almost no explicit boy/girl relationships; but the sometimes exotic settings, the evident privilege in the boarding school clientele and the basic relationships depicted in the schoolgirl or schoolboy world, continue to hold interest, particularly for girls.

Adventure stories

The word 'adventure' suggests action, suspense, challenge, adversaries, adversities and excitement. When the word is applied to stories it also implies a safe return to normality and covers most children's books in that most of the ingredients can be found in fairy stories, fantasy, historical fiction, school stories, in family stories and other broad categories of fiction.

From earliest times adventure stories have brought interest and excitement to people in many countries in the myths and legends and folk tales; later in stories like *Robinson Crusoe, Gulliver's Travels* and *Treasure Island*; and recently in the wealth of modern stories that provide a venturing out of the known into the unknown with all the uncertainty, fear, anticipation and excitement that such a step can bring.

Adventure in the past brings the genre into an overlap with historical fiction and adventure in the future aligns with much science fiction, but the term 'adventure story' is generally applied to the book that depicts a child or gang of children who become involved in a situation where they need to tackle a difficult problem or person, solve a mystery, undertake a journey or right a wrong. This is often done without the presence of parents or authority, though there may be kindly adults around who help where needed. The adversary is often adult and part of the interest for children lies in this fact and in the eventual triumphing over adversary and adversity.

As adventure is such an encompassing term so adventures can be experienced in most settings, land, sea, in the air, in space or underground. Armstrong Sperry's *The Boy Who Was Afraid* is a challenge of the sea, as is R. L. Stevenson's *Treasure Island* and Willard Price's *Underwater Adventure*. The air is the scene of Ivan Southall's *To the Wild Sky* in which a group of children flying in a light aircraft across Australia have to cope with the situation when the pilot dies in mid-flight, and W. C. Johns' *Biggles* books portrayed an adult pilot in exciting situations. Andre Norton's *Iron Cage* contains laboratory children on a strange planet. While Jules Verne's *Journey to the Centre of the Earth* takes a fanciful look at the inside of earth, Colin Thiele's *Chadwick's Chimney* is a mystery in underground caves in Australia.

There are many such books for children and many that make from the ingredients an easily absorbed story in which the reader races along with the action. This is the appeal of the phenomenal Enid Blyton books, dozens of which are adventure stories concerning the Famous Five and the Secret Seven in books like *Five on a Treasure Island, The Island of Adventure, Castle of Adventure*, and so on. Her books have been best-sellers since the 1940s and are read by children all over the world, despite the very English characters and settings. Similarly, the *Hardy Boys* of American origin have maintained their popularity over the years for much the same reasons of simplicity, action, and familiarity because of the quantity.

Adventure stories often centre on school holidays, an obvious choice because not only are children out of their normal school routine but are often out of their normal setting and are thus conveniently open to the possibility of the unusual.

Some adventure stories involve a mystery or a crime, to be solved by the detective work of the child or group, eventually bringing the criminal to justice. Some adventures are the result of war and there are many excellent books that treat both war and adventure in a way that grips the reader with suspense. Examples include two in which children journey across Europe to find parents from whom they were separated by war; Ian Serraillier's *The Silver Sword* and Ann Holm's *I am David*. Meindert de Jong's *House of Sixty Fathers* shows a small boy separated from his family during the Japanese invasion of China in the Second World War.

Books that look at the dangers and excitements of a child's life in wartime include Christine Nöstlinger's *Fly Away Home*, set in Vienna in Austria and Robert Westall's *The Machine Gunners* set in Tyneside in northern England, all during the Second World War.

The adventure story seems to translate well across national boundaries and languages, and a foreign setting is not often a barrier to enjoyment. The English child can enjoy Andrew Salkey's *Hurricane*, set in the West Indies; the Jamaican child reads Willard Price's books; the American child is engrossed in *I am David* in Europe and Australia's *Walkabout* by James Vance Marshall has an international readership. Childhood *is* adventure, and challenge and change are part of everyday life for most children in whatever country.

But whether the story adventure is urban, rural, seaborne or airborne it is usually fraught with danger, either actual or potential, involves resourcefulness and sometimes courage. The interplay of characters reveals the strengths and weaknesses of the group or the individual child, and the ending indicates the successful completion of the journey, the solving of the mystery, the tying up of the threads of the story, the end of the adventure.

Family stories

Trends in family stories reflect the trends in families. The early books on a family theme were of the kind exemplified by Louisa Alcott's *Little Women* where there was a close relationship between parents and each child, a togetherness in thought and action and a comforting feeling that whatever misfortune might befall parent or child, underneath and roundabout was the security of the supportive family.

Whether or not all real children's families were like that, the family story nevertheless provided a satisfying emotional warmth. Similar pictures of family life are seen in Laura

Ingalls Wilder's *Little House on the Prairie*, E. Nesbit's *The Railway Children*, Eleanor Estes' stories of the Moffat family, Elizabeth Enright's Melendy family in *The Saturdays* and the close-knit family in Joan Lingard's books in Scottish settings, such as *The Clearance*.

But in the 1960s there was a gradual introduction of the idea that not all families were close-knit, nor complete. The possibility of a 'live-in' mother and parental arguments is seen in John Rowe Townsend's *Gumbie's Yard*, marital discord in Erich Kästner's *Lottie and Lisa* and William Mayne's *Blue Boat*. Adoption into a family is seen in comforting terms in *Anne of Green Gables* by L. M. Montgomery, still well loved by children.

The disruption of family life is shown in Paula Fox's *How Many Miles to Babylon?*, a black boy's distress when his mother goes into hospital, and in Bernard Ashley's *The Trouble With Donovan Croft*, who is put into foster-care when his mother has to return to Jamaica temporarily from London.

In the 1970s and early 1980s there developed a literature for children on the theme of the family with a handicapped child. There are excellent examples of picture book stories such as Camilla Jessell's *Mark's Wheelchair Adventures* and Diana Peter's *Claire and Emma*, which is about deaf sisters. There are books for the young reader such as Susan Burke's *Alexander in Trouble* who amazes himself and his family with what he can do in and out of his wheelchair. There are books for the older reader in which the family's relationship with a handicapped child is shown to involve each member of the family, as in Colby Rodowsky's *What About Me?* where a teenage girl has mixed feelings about her mongol brother, and Eleanor Spence's *The October Child* where the main character is autistic.

Then there are books which depict the discord between parent and child and between brother and sister as part of the natural day-to-day conversation and disagreement of family life, as in Louise Fitzhugh's story *Nobody's Family is Going to Change*, in which eleven-year-old Emma and her black American family disagree on what she and her brother should be and do. Family discord is seen too in some teenage novels discussed later, a discord which stems from the fact that teenage is the departure point from dependence to independence, though fictional (and real) parents differ on when and how the vital step is taken.

The family story in western countries has changed from the 'wholeness' of the early books to the treatment of the family as individuals, sometimes in conflict with other individuals in the family; from the standard unit of mother, father, children and often grandparents and extended family, to the family as the child and whoever happens to be sharing his life with him at home. There are exceptions but in general, at the time of writing, modern stories of a united family are few, despite modern children's enjoyment of the earlier family stories and their translation to the film screen.

Realism

Arthur Koestler suggests that the distinction between fantasy and reality is a 'late acquisition of rational thought'. The young child who has not yet developed sufficient knowledge and experience to know what is true and what is false or what is real and what is unreal, often finds the two interchangeable and moves happily between them.

For example there are many children who have an 'imaginary' friend who is very 'real' to them, but there are also many adults who get so involved in a television series that they 'believe' the characters are 'real' and send abusive or sympathetic letters, or accost the actors in the street. The inability to make the distinction indicates that many people do not acquire a sufficient capacity for rational thought as they grow out of childhood.

There is a thin dividing line between fantasy and reality, a point made in Aidan Chambers' *Breaktime* in which both the author and the characters explore that theme. But the realism referred to in this section is not dividing books into those that can be called fantasy and those we can term realistic. It is a recognition that the reality to which we relate is not necessarily a matter of time, place or character, but of the basic needs we feel. So realism is not always a blow-by-blow description of the everyday reality involved in factual and situation realism, it is also the presence of factors with which the reader can identify emotionally, those that cause the reader to think, 'That's how *I* feel' and which are thus real to him.

Realism can be divided into several areas of which six are listed here:

1. *Factual realism*; as in historical novels, stories of other lands, science fiction, career novels, and the coverage of factually important aspects in other forms of children's literature.
2. *Situation realism*; where the settings may be in an identifiable location and the characters of an identifiable age and social stratum and where the whole treatment makes the situation believable.
3. *Emotional realism*; where the psychological, personal and emotional effect of the facts and the situation must ring true. The way people react to each other emotionally in the story can be a telling comment on a personal relationship in 'real' life even though the reader has not personally experienced it in that particular form. The depiction of certain emotions are often taboo in children's books. Until recently death was avoided or glossed over, but the death of an animal or an old person is common to children in all countries; death by illness or accident is known to most; the death of

people in war is within the experience of all too many unfortunate children; and most children know of all of these by television, newspapers or adult conversation, if not by personal experience.

But emotions are concerned also with happy aspects of mind, thought and action and the realistic fictional presentation of love, joy and hope are as valid as that of fear, grief and hate.

4. *Social realism*; which tends to be equated with the 'kitchen sink' aspects of life in both adult and children's books. 'Telling it like it is' often refers to aspects like drugs, sex, violence, political and adverse social conditions, poverty, racial and class problems, handicaps, and family discord. But social, in the sense of 'of society' encompasses the brighter aspects also of communication, community care, children helping each other, families, enjoyable school and home activities, leisure pursuits, multi-ethnic projects, children overcoming handicaps.

Society can be as broad as the country in which a child lives or as narrow and localized as the street or the school. The norms may be the same or they may conflict, but both are real to the child in that society.

5. *Illustrative realism*; whether in picture book or in the illustrations to story books, realism can be seen in the way the artist portrays the *essence* of a scene, an event, a person, to transmit and extend the feeling of reality obtained from the text. Reality is not always attained by photographic illustration nor by faithful reproduction in a painting. The true artist perceives the real under the layers of disguise or decoration and is able by simple outline or rich detail to make it real for the reader.

6. *Realism for the reading-retarded child*; the use of realistic setting and vocabulary in books for the backward or

retarded reader can be supported for a number of reasons, based largely on the technical aspects of learning to read. When we read we are not only identifying the letters and the words as pronounceable and defining the meaning of the word, we are selecting the meaning given to those words by the author, within the context. We are also assigning the meaning which our own experience of the word has given us. The more familiar with the situation described by the word, the better we understand the text. It then becomes easier to find meaning in what we read and we are more motivated to do it again, thus gaining practice and increasing reading skill. The handicapped child who for physical or mental reasons is behind the able child in reading ability, or the child who is reading-retarded for social or emotional reasons, tends to have had a limited experience. He will find familiarity in stories that describe what he *has* experienced, whether it is physically, geographically or emotionally real. This aids his reading, gives him a feeling of achievement in successfully completing a book or a story, and encourages him to continue to make the effort with books.

Realism in books is man's relationship with man, the characters' reactions to society, society in manageable proportions. Real life is a form of education and of bibliotherapy. An Rutgers van der Loeff has said that real issues in contemporary settings are 'a ripening experience'.

Many writers say that they put themselves in their characters' places – what if I found myself in this situation? – pregnant as in Gunnel Beckman's *Mia*, jealous of my sister as in Pamela Rogers's *The Stone Angel*, worried about chemical warfare as in John Branfield's *Nancecuke*, hating school as in K. M. Peyton's *Pennington's Seventeenth Summer*, caged in by high rise flats as in Charles Keeping's *Charlie,*

Charlotte and the Golden Canary, bullied by fellow boys as in Betsy Byars' *The Eighteenth Emergency*, or uplifted by first love as in Beverley Cleary's *Fifteen*; overwhelmed by the beauty of a scene, the wonder of a spider, the immensity of the marvellous world, as in Maria Gripe's *Hugo*, safe in the security of a loving relationship as in Honor Arundel's books, overcoming a handicap as in Ivan Southall's *Let the Balloon Go*.

In years gone by children were shielded from the unpleasant issues in life or were amongst them, but now, as never before, many children throughout the world, though living in a small unit of society, are aware of the big issues and indeed may be affected by them. Young people in teenage are particularly aware and vulnerable in both personal and communal issues and this is discussed in the section on teenage books.

But for the average child there is a progression towards a larger understanding of society and his place in it, and realistic treatment of themes in children's books can both mirror and aid that progression.

Teenage books
Although other age groups in the years before adulthood are rarely assigned their own literature, because reading age is not always the same as chronological age, there has developed a literature for readers of teenage, either written specifically for the age and the needs of the age or on themes which attract the teenage reader. The attention given to these books and readers in libraries and schools has helped to promote reading amongst young people at a time when reading normally declines.

Teenage can be a vulnerable period in which physiological maturity may not coincide with social or emotional maturity, and intellectual maturity is a much later and rarer development.

Social conditions in western countries in the 1960s and 1970s led to a working teenage population with time and money, a ready market for commercial commodities, and an entry into the working adult's life without the working adult's responsibilities. In addition many teenagers still in full-time education had parents who were more affluent than in previous periods. This produced a situation not found in many other countries, where the transition from childhood to adulthood was and is, made by means of a ceremony, and although the young people are teenaged chronologically, they are either children or adults in their societies. So reading material for teenagers tends to be found in those countries where there is a recognized transition period in which the teenaged person is gradually, legally, socially and emotionally eased into adulthood.

There are available certain kinds of book which can be categorized in the following ways;

1 The teenage novel
2. Series for teenage readers
3. Career stories
4. Adult fiction preferred by teenage readers.

Reading interests are discussed in Chapter Seven where the whole range of needs and preferences are detailed.

1. The teenage novel

This genre can be defined as fiction written specifically with teenage readers in mind rather than those many adult novels adopted by teenagers. Many teenagers do read adult novels from the early part of teenage and most surveys show that twelve-year-old girls read the light romantic and historical novels and the clear-cut detective stories of writers like Agatha Christie, while boys of thirteen or so are often reading the adventure stories of writers like Ian Fleming and Alistair MacLean.

But the teenage novel began in the USA in the 1960s and in Britain and Scandinavia in the 1970s. It has developed to the point where it would be possible to divide it into sub-categories –

a. by age; suitable for early teenage, middle teenage or young adult,
b. by theme; love, adventure, protest against war/crime/adult oppression, coming to terms with failure/success/death/handicap, accepting that independence brings responsibility etc. etc.
c. by reading/conceptual ability; books for the good reader, the able but reluctant reader, the less-able reader.
d. format; e.g. one-off novels, series, picture books for teenagers.

The teenage novel fills a need for books for those young people who have grown out of children's books but cannot yet cope with adult books, attracting also those who are able to read but are reluctant to spend time reading. It provides the next stepping stone for the less-able reader to progress to after the series books for less-able teenagers and it is found interesting by those young people who are reading adult books but who enjoy the teenage novel because it is more directly concerned with their interests and age group.

The appeal lies in the fact that the teenage novel has characters of a similar chronological age to the reader, in situations that both conceptually and emotionally 'speak' to the minds and hearts of the teenager. For instance Gunnel Beckmann's *Mia* is not about a pregnant girl, it is about a girl who realizes that her suspected pregnancy affects her family, her friends, her schooling and her future. Paul Zindel's *The Pigman* is concerned with two teenagers whose practical joke leads them to befriend an old man and to unwittingly destroy him, a novel of a dawning sense of responsibility.

81

Beverley Cleary's *Fifteen*, though dated now in some respects, nevertheless continues to hold a strong appeal for young people with its theme of first love.

There are hundreds of books with teenage characters, living and working with each other and with adults, finding their way through the challenges, uncertainties, sorrows and joys of adolescence and presenting a wide-screen picture of the whole age range from 12 to 20 in a variety of countries, with sad and happy endings. A literary critic has said that 'a large part of adolescence consists of a magnified awareness of the singularity of one's own situation'. Many of the teenage novels showing individuals in contemporary society in effect provide some counterbalance to that feeling of being the only person this has ever happened to, the only one who feels like this. The teenage novel shows clearly that others have been there before you.

At a time of transition from childhood to adulthood, the teenage novel can be a bridge.

2. Series for teenagers

These are publishers' series that put individual titles under a collective heading in order to make it easier for parents, teachers, librarians and readers to pinpoint the books that appeal to the teenage reader.

In some cases the books are written specifically for the series, in others the books are already published in hardback but the paperback edition is marketed under a series banner. In some series there is an age or an ability specification, and in others the books are simply those, both fiction and non-fiction for children, teenagers or adults, that are thought to appeal to the teenage reader.

For the able reader in Britain and overseas there are series like the excellent Bodley Head *Books for New Adults* in hardback, Macmillan Educational's *Topliners* in paperback, Ward Lock Educational's *Short Stories*, with titles like

Sports Stories and *Love Stories*; Hodder and Stoughton's paperback series *Black Knight* and Heinemann's hardback series for reluctant readers *Pyramids*. Collins' *Lions*, Penguin's *Puffins* and the Longman's *Imprint Books* all contain titles that appeal to teenagers.

In the USA there are, equally, many publishers such as Dell, Bantam Books, Avon, Pocket Books and *The New American Library* producing paperback titles for teenagers.

Generally such series are packaged in colour covers, with distinctive format and logo and are an identifiable aid to selection, quality and appeal.

Series for the less-able readers are more numerous, particularly in Britain. There are some one hundred and fifty series for the learner reader, with a total of around 2,000 titles. Most are graded reading books but there are approximately thirty series specifically aimed at the reading-retarded teenager and sufficiently general to be considered as books rather than reading texts.

The term less-able reader is usual but backward, reading-retarded and remedial are other commonly used terms. The term can be applied to the reader who is a year or more behind the norm for the age, or to the young teenager or adult who has a reading age of less than 9.

In recent years more attention has been paid to this latter group, as in many countries the need for greater literacy has caused educationists and librarians to press for reading materials suited to the age and interests of the teenager and adult. Many were otherwise condemned to learn from text and pictures intended for the young child, with consequent psychological inhibitions, lack of motivation and of relevance. Whatever the cause of reading-retardation, whether physical, emotional, mental or social, first language or second language, many countries have large numbers of young people and adults who need books covering both pictorially and textually matters of interest, with simplified controlled vocabulary and with eye-catching and informative illustrations to aid comprehension.

Examples of attractive and enjoyable stories can be found in series such as Nelson's *Getaways*, Methuen's *Forward*, Cassell's *Club, Banjo, Disco*, Evans' *Checkers*, Hart Davis' *Solos*, Collins' *'Help'*, Heinemann's *Joan Tate Books*, Longman's *Knockouts* (in both text and picture strip format), and some of Benn's *Inner Ring* books.

All these and many other publishers' series have teenage or adult characters in situations relevant to many teenagers, while other series for less-able younger children have particular books that would be suitable because they are concerned with aspects of interest to all ages, such as animals, information, sport and true stories.

Again the usefulness of series for teenage and adult less-able readers lies in the fact that they bring together titles which might otherwise be lost amongst the large number of publications available. Such series can save time, provide a body of reading material and, most importantly, can offer the reading-retarded person a chance of success and enjoyment in reading.

Two organizations in Britain have published guides to suitable material: *Take Off . . .* by Jenny Armour, (London, Library Association, 1980), and *Starting Point; books for the illiterate adult and older reluctant reader*, edited by Sue Brownhill, (London, National Book League, 1979).

3. Career stories
These are often a mixture of school story, light romance and job information. The best should contain factual information about entry to and duties in a particular career, set in a digestible fictional form. But many authors find it difficult to create interesting characters and activities within the confines of the career information. Others set such information into a glamourized background or plot, such as the *Sue Bar-*

ton novels by Helen Boylston which are stories rather than nursing information career books, while Nancy Martin's *Four Girls in a Store* manages to combine plot with information.

There is a place on the shelves for such books in that they can provide a general background picture and perhaps spark an interest in a career not previously considered.

4. Adult fiction for teenage readers

As indicated in the chapter on children's reading interests some children begin to read adult fiction and non-fiction at an early age while keeping up their interest in children's books. Usually adult books chosen in early teenage have a straightforward story with clearly defined characters and action on themes such as adventure, romance, mystery and ghosts.

These themes continue to attract throughout teenage and into adulthood, but for some teenagers the more 'literary' novel begins to offer satisfaction. In the Whitehead survey of *Children and Their Books*, the names of authors of adult books claimed to have been read by the teenagers surveyed included, for example, Asimov, Barstow, Bradbury, Braine, Bronte, Buchan, Chandler, Conrad, Dickens, Drabble, Golding, Graves, Hemingway, Huxley, James, D. H. Lawrence, Somerset Maugham, Mary McCarthy, Henry Miller, Monserrat, O'Brien, Orwell, Pasternak, Rattigan, Sagan, Sartre, Sayers, Scott, Shute, Simenon, C. P. Snow, Solzhenitsyn, Steinbeck, Thurber, Tolstoy, Waugh, Wells, Wilde, Angus Wilson, Woolf and Zola.

Also named were numerous 'popular' authors such as Agatha Christie, Catherine Cookson, James Herriot, Alfred Hitchcock, Ian Fleming, Alistair MacLean, Eric Segal and John Wyndham.

It is clear also that those female teenagers who continue to read voluntarily after growing out of children's books, and they are in the minority, read widely amongst the popular adult literature and magazines, while male teenagers read more non-fiction and are interested in a narrower range of periodicals. But detailed discussion of the subject of teenage reading is given in my book *Libraries and Literature for Teenagers* (London, Deutsch, 1975), and descriptions and suggestions of books can be found in G. Robert Carlsen's *Books and the Teenage Reader; a guide for teachers, librarians and parents*, (N.Y., Harper & Row, 2nd ed. 1980).

Poetry

Many children find enjoyment, information, new words, fresh thoughts and the possibility of participation in the rhythm of poetry. As the child grows his awareness can be increased by a turn of phrase, a word, or a poem that encapsulates a deep meaning. When the reader's mind grasps the capsule it bursts, to spread the fragrance, the delight, the knowledge and the self awareness or insight. This can be achieved of course in prose, but the 'special effects' of poetry lie in the sense of rhythm and, when well done, in rhyme; in the poetic imagery; in language that crystallizes thoughts, actions and events.

The length of a poem is appropriate to the concentration span of any reader but the comprehension of the concepts in a poem depends not only upon the ability of the poet to convey them but also upon the kind of mind the reader brings to the poem.

For the very young, nursery rhymes form an introduction to poetry. The rhymes and rhythms, alliteration, humour, the sounds of words, have caused them to remain part of each generation's childhood ever since the early origins of nursery rhymes. Many were social and political comment on events and practices of the day; some were and are baby-handling aids, and all are a means of sharing and communicating between parent and child or other person and child.

While Iona and Peter Opie's *The Oxford Nursery Rhyme Book* is the definitive work with its 800 rhymes and 600 illustrations, the books with greater child appeal include Raymond Briggs' masterly *The Mother Goose Treasury*, with hundreds of rhymes and very effective illustrative content and layout, and Peggy Blakeley's 92-verse selection *The Great Big Book of Nursery Rhymes*, illustrated by Frank Francis. There are numerous short compilations and some translations of other countries' traditions as in N. M. Bodecker's picture book *It's Raining Said John Twaining*; *Danish Nursery Rhymes*.

Humorous poetry is popular throughout the age range. I mentioned it in the section on humour but can add here the appeal to older children and young people of books like Spike Milligan's own *Silly Verse for Kids*, William Cole's *Oh, What Nonsense* and T. S. Eliot's *Old Possum's Book of Practical Cats*.

Most anthologies of poetry, whether on general or specific themes, are the selection of a compiler or editor and thus an individual's personal choice. This can give either a wholeness to the selection because the selector shows clear taste or a clear objective in the choice, or it can make the selection fragmentary and idiosyncratic. When volumes of poetry are considered for library purchase or class use criteria similar to that used for fiction can be employed; the content (or plot); the language; the style in terms of rhythm and devices; the intended reader in terms of interest, age and ability; the intended use by teacher, storyteller and child.

The range and number of poets included in the anthology can be gauged from the index, contents list or author index. The nature of the poems may be seen in the arrangement into subject sections. The presence of illustration may be a help or a hindrance depending upon whether it is an integral part of the book in quantity, quality and style; whether it is simply there to break up the potentially dull appearance of pages of poetry; or is intended to be page decoration.

Examples of useful anthologies include Kaye Webb's *I Like This Poem*, an anthology resulting from children's own choice; Louis Untermeyer's *The Golden Treasury of Poetry*; Edward Blishen's *Oxford Book of Poetry For Children*, illustrated by Brian Wildsmith, and for the older end of the age range, collections like Geoffrey Summerfield's *Voices* and *The New American Poetry* edited by Donald M. Allen.

Volumes of poetry by individual poets tend to be less popular but are often packaged in attractive format, offering an aesthetic appeal in addition to the value of the poetic content. Examples here include British poets' work such as R. L. Stevenson's *A Child's Garden of Verses*; A. A. Milne's *The Christopher Robin Verse Book*; Charles Causely's *Collected Poems*; Ted Hughes' *Moon-bells and Other Poems*, and the work of American poets such as David McCord's *Far and Few*, and Langston Hughes' *Don't You Turn Back*.

The subject content in poetry is as varied and interesting as that in fiction and non-fiction – the whole of human knowledge being eligible for poetic inspiration. Thus there is nonsense, fairy, fantasy, adventure, animal, nature, realistic, war, rural, urban, political, satirical, romantic, religious, introspective, philosophical and descriptive poetry that can be read by and read to children throughout the age range.

Children's own poetry

It is common for many children to lose their enjoyment of poetry as they grow older. It may be that the quantity of other forms of reading material and imaginative experience compete with poetry for the child's attention, or it may be that the *study* of poetry in school leads to the attitude that poetry is a difficult school subject, a task rather than an experience.

A change in children's creative writing is also seen as children grow older. For some years I have been a member of the panel of judges for the annual W. H. Smith's *Children As Writers* Award, and have marvelled at the fresh, original inspirational poetry of many children in the five to eight age group. The work of children in the nine to twelve range shows the hand of teachers who require a whole class to write a poem on 'snow' or 'my body' or 'the sea'. Would-be poets in the thirteen to sixteen age range tend to be derivative and intensely self-conscious and guilty of striving for either stylistic or subject content effect. The truly original and poetic entries are fewer than for the youngest age group. Nevertheless thousands of entries are received each year and the best are published in book form in *Children As Writers*, along with the best prose entries, witnessing to the continuing interest of teachers and children in the literary, intellectual and inspirational aspects of poetry.

Information books or non-fiction

Factual books written specifically for young people form part of the total range called children's literature. In the chapter on selection there is an outline of the criteria for selecting information books and a discussion of the importance of looking at the use to which the book may be put in terms of answering questions of varying complexity.

This section is a more general appraisal of non-fiction, general because there are thousands of children's information books and hundreds of adult information books adopted by children and young people. Information can be obtained in a number of different formats which can be listed in the following way;

Annual reports
Blue prints
Books
Charts

Clippings or cuttings
Correspondence
Graphs
Kits
Manuscripts
Maps
Music
Newspapers
Pamphlets
Patents
Periodicals
Photographs
Plans
Reports
Theses
Trade catalogues
Audio-visual media

While recognizing the necessity for each of these as a medium appropriate to information-finding by young people, for the purposes of this book comment is confined to the book format, omitting school textbooks. All textbooks are information books but not all information books are textbooks.

Information books are not usually mere collections of facts but contain fact, concept and attitude and each of these should be examined in order to determine accuracy, vocabulary, scope and author bias or enthusiasm, for there are trends in information books as there are in children's fiction. In recent years emphasis has been laid on the following:

1. Visual appeal; by the use of varying sizes from pocket book to magazine size; by glossy covers; colour illustration; the development of picture dictionaries and illustrated encyclopaedias; and pop-up and pull-out features.

2. Whole approach; books of a composite nature presenting situations looking at contributory factors rather than the traditional one-topic book with demarcation between subjects.

3. Research approach; planned to be used and thus contains index, signposting, captions to pictures, further readings and other aids to ease of use.

4. Series; these may be designed for age groups, activity use, school project or topic work, individual browsing, basic introductions to themes or in-depth coverage of themes. Whatever the publishers' intentions there are large quantities of series available, differing widely and varying in quality and usefulness even within a series. Each volume in each series needs to be examined rather than making an assumption that the whole series is of equal worth.

5. Subject content; the difference between books for younger and books for older children lies in the level of coverage rather than in the choice of theme. There are very simple books on computers or trade unions (Ladybird and Dinosaur publications) for the young reader or the less able older reader, themes which some years ago would have been considered of no interest or beyond the mental grasp of young children.

Information books may be in the form of a quick reference book or descriptive or discursive book, with the emphasis on text or the emphasis on illustration. Reference books are those to which the reader refers for a particular piece of information and are organized in such a way as to facilitate that search. Atlases, dictionaries, encyclopaedias and yearbooks are examples of this kind of book and it is necessary to check the level of knowledge contained in each, the currency of the information, that is its up-to-dateness, and *how* to extract the information. Using such reference books involves alphabetical skill, ability to determine the correct keyword, to understand the symbols or codes in atlases and dictionaries, index skill in using heavy type and cross referencing, understanding the way the information is arranged, evaluating the scope of the content and assessing its usefulness to the reader's requirement.

Descriptive or discursive books on a theme or number of themes may be useful for leisure reading or for some kinds of schoolwork. Some information books, particularly on the subjects of history or geography, take a documentary approach using original source material, or a human interest approach, setting the period or place into the context of a real or a fictional child.

Some scientific and natural history books take an experimental approach, enabling the reader to understand by both reading and doing. Biography varies between at one extreme, the straightforward chronological description of people who have influenced the course of events and, at the other extreme, the glossy glamorized depiction of famous people.

In all the kinds of information book the treatment may be largely pictorial, largely textual or an equal mixture of the two. A glance at many information books reveals the difference between those books in which the pictures inform visually and those in which the pictures are merely decoration for the topic; between those in which the illustrations or photographs are crammed with detail not relevant to the theme and those in which they concentrate on the important features of the topic.

Photo books have already been mentioned under the heading of picture books, where some of the 'first' books for young children are pages of full colour photographs with or without captions or text. These are mainly intended to provide informative pictures to identify objects or people and to stimulate language by means of encouraging the child to name what is seen and then to talk to himself about it or with the accompanying adult.

Increasingly information books are appearing in photo book form with explanatory text, the intention here being to offer children in the middle and older sections of the age range, pictorial information from which the reader can pick out the specific aspects according to his requirements while obtaining an overall visual impression from the total illustration. Also available are art books in photographic form and large numbers of activity books in which the reader is shown how to do or make particular things through the various stages depicted in the photographs.

Publishers are beginning to be aware that pictorial information has to be planned and edited in the same way as text, and there are, increasingly, information books in which the illustrations do give information in their own right, via content, the use of colour where appropriate and via the placing of illustrations in relation to the text.

Whatever the subject content the books may have a serious or a lighthearted treatment, for a young or an older reader, in pictorial or textual form, in descriptive or prescriptive style, with glance or analytical coverage, in quick reference or depth reading organization, in attractive or dull packaging, in the same way as adult non-fiction.

But it is important for the child reader to have access to this range of treatment so that his varying needs and interests are catered for and so that he has an opportunity not only to be informed factually, but extended, through seeing the author's perception of that branch of knowledge.

I have visited several countries where information books, as opposed to textbooks, were not readily available. This can be explained in two ways. First the education system in those countries relies heavily on a rigid syllabus, textbooks, teacher-centred learning, and examinations, leaving no time and no need for the wide ranging or specific information books used in, for example, Britain, for topic work, projects, self learning and assessed work. Thus the lack of an educational market discourages publishers from producing information books.

This in turn creates the second factor for their absence from libraries; that such books are not published in any quantity and few are available in translation, therefore libraries cannot stock what is not obtainable.

Yet another reason is apparent in some countries where the climate and work and social customs put reading low as a leisure-time priority whether fiction or non-fiction.

As mentioned in the chapter on reading interests, surveys show that boys read more non-fiction than girls and that for both boys and girls such reading is not the school-subject information but that connected with their hobbies, with sport, animals, transport, nature, science and famous people. Surveys also show that the gifted child often reads voraciously amongst non-fiction rather than fiction. The less-able teenage reader can often cope better with non-fiction on subjects that personally interest him and this fact is used to good effect in much of the material created for literacy programmes.

Information books in the school library, the public library and the home are providers of knowledge and knowledge for school purposes, for personal interest or even knowledge for its own sake, is necessary for the intellectual, social and emotional development of all children.

Further readings
Aldiss, Brian. *The True History of Science Fiction*. New York, Doubleday, 1973
Bettelheim, Bruno. *The Uses of Enchantment*; *the meaning and importance of fairy tales*. New York, Knopf, 1976
Blount, Margaret. *Animal Land; the creatures of children's fiction*. London, Hutchinson, 1974

Carlsen, G. Robert. *Books and the Teenage Reader*. New York, Harper & Row, 1980

Cook, Elizabeth. *The Ordinary and the Fabulous*. London, C.U.P., 1976

Fisher, Margery. *Intent Upon Reading*. London, Brockhampton, 1964,

Matters of Fact; aspects of non-fiction for children. London, Brockhampton, 1972

Who's Who in Children's Books; a treasury of the familiar characters of childhood. London, Weidenfeld & Nicholson, 1975

Frizzell Smith, Dorothy and Andrews, Eva L. *Subject Index to Poetry for Children and Young People, 1957–1975*. Chicago, A.L.A. 1977

Marshall, M. R. *Libraries and Literature for Teenagers*. London, Deutsch, 1975

Marshall, M. R. *Libraries and the Handicapped Child*. London, Deutsch, 1981

Ray, Sheila. *The Blyton Phenomenon*. London, Deutsch, 1982,

Children's Fiction. London, Brockhampton, 1970

Sutherland, Zena and Arbuthnot, May Hill. *Children and Books*. New York, Scott, Foresman, 5th ed. 1975

Wehmeyer, Lillian Biermann. *Images in a Crystal Ball; world futures in novels for young people*. New York, Libraries Unlimited, 1981

Children's Literature in Education

Hornbook Magazine

Signal

CHAPTER SIX

Illustration and Children's Books

The importance of pictures in the life of human beings is demonstrated from the earliest times. Man has always communicated visually. Cave paintings, sign writing, art, sculpture, film, television and recently holovision, are pictorial forms of communication, expressing messages, concepts, objects, information and imagination. Some written languages in the world are picture based, such as Japanese and Chinese. Even when we speak we use hand pictures to describe size, shape or emotion, sometimes using these where words cannot adequately express what we want to describe, as with 'circle' or 'spiral', or the visual body language of raised eyebrows, shrug of the shoulders, or 'hands up'.

From birth the sense of sight is stimulated and research has shown that a baby left lying flat in a cot or pram when awake does not learn as quickly as one who is put into a position to see what is going on around. The child carried around on mother's back may thus learn more, earlier, of immediate use in everyday life. Through sight the identifying, classifying and categorizing that enable people to make sense and order begins in babyhood and develops throughout life.

So human beings are accustomed to giving and receiving information both formally and informally by means of sight, vision and pictures. It has been suggested that 90% of what we learn is learned by sight and we tend to remember what we have seen. The old saying 'seeing is believing' is still largely true today, despite the increased knowledge of scientific aspects of visual perception and despite recognition that brilliant techniques of photography can deceive the eye.

The child in the technologically developed countries of the world has been used to a high standard of visual presentation of information but children in other societies were and are not so fortunate. Children in the early days of children's literature in England responded to the woodcuts and engravings in some of the first books for children though such pictures were often decorative rather than strictly related to the story of information. The introduction of colour by hand painting gave rise to the description 'penny plain and tuppence coloured' for marketing purposes, until the invention of colour lithography enabled children's books to be produced with colour printed illustrations. Kate Greenaway's work, commemorated in the annual Kate Greenaway Award for outstanding illustrations in children's books in the UK, exemplifies the change from the black and white woodcuts, engravings and drawings to the possibilities for full colour with all that that implies in terms of attraction, imagination, artistic scope, and, particularly important to child development, the kinds of information that a colour picture imparts that a black and white picture cannot.

The latest printing and colour printing techniques allow tremendous scope for both artist and book designer in content and format, facilitating most methods from charcoal to water colour, from collage to photography, and computer drawings. High technology enables the book and its pictures to be transmitted to another medium of vision via film as in the films and filmstrips using the picture book's pictures; or via equipment such as epidiascopes and other magnifying equipment like *Visualtek* which magnify the book page on to a screen or visual display unit.

The 'visualizing' of children's book illustration via the television screen in dramatization or straightforward storytelling, as in the BBC's *Jackanory* programme, also demonstrates the versatility of and the importance attached to, the pictorial content of children's books.

Pictorial content is not only that found in picture books but the illustrations used in story books, in information books, in picture reference books, in picture strip and comic books, in paper engineering or pop-up books, because all have a place in the reading diet of children of all ages and all purport to serve a purpose. What is the purpose?

It can be one or more of the following:

1. To decorate the pages as part of the total book design
2. To enhance the text
3. To interpret the text
4. To increase visual perception
5. To provide visual information
6. To aid visual discrimination
7. To externalize, pictorially, fears that cannot be expressed in words
8. To tell the story (in books with and without words)

If these purposes are achieved then the result may also include aesthetic appreciation and enjoyment. But the methods by which these are all achieved revolve round factors such as:

1. Graphic style of the artist; the medium used, e.g. line, pencil, oils, collage, full colour; and the originality, vitality, humour and emotional power.
2. Sympathy with the text; matching the mood/colour/historical period/emotion of the text with line, colour and content emphasis in the illustration.
3. Content; relates to the single concept per picture or per page or the profusely detailed picture, chosen by the illustrator as suitably representative and descriptive of the textual content, and interpreted in such a way as to accurately portray the text while extending the viewer's knowledge and perception pictorially; how the illustrator makes the pictures tell the story.

4. Relevance to the child's perception and experience e.g. preferably not abstract art or half shapes for young children.
5. Layout in relationship to the text in order to ensure that
    a. the illustration is on the page of the text to which it refers
    b. it is placed logically on that page
    c. it conforms to the legibility requirements, e.g. preferably not overprinted on the text.
6. Layout of the book in design terms; cover, page design, typeface, illustration, end papers etc.
7. Use of colour where appropriate because colour is an information provider, offering attraction and information, enabling objects and people to be better identified, though black and white pictures are acceptable if they clearly delineate the matter depicted.

As indicated earlier, many kinds of children's book contain illustrations, the most obvious being the picture book.

Picture books
The 32-page picture book is the most usual form and is generally intended for the young child. At the youngest age the picture book may be used by adults for reading to and sharing with the child. The pictures are therefore likely to be more important than the text in that they become a conversation piece with the adult elaborating on the text, confirming it, reinforcing it, testing it with the child, usually as a natural part of communication. This is true of the nursery rhyme books in which the words are usually felt rather than understood by the child; the rhythm of the words and the visual interest of the picture being more important. Two examples of the words of nursery rhymes will indicate that a child's comprehension of the meaning is most unlikely, but the rhythm and sound, and probably actions, are paramount.

99

> See-saw Margery Daw
> Johnny shall have a new master
> He shall have but a penny a day
> Because he can't go any faster.

and

> Moses supposes his toeses are roses
> But Moses supposes erroneously
> For nobody's toeses are posies of roses
> As Moses supposes his toeses to be.

One of the best collections, from an illustration viewpoint, is the *Mother Goose Treasury* of Raymond Briggs, who spent over two years selecting the rhymes, planning the page layout and drawing and painting the illustrations. His perception of both design layout and rhyme content are unequalled as yet. Jack and Jill are given a double spread with an enormous green hill down which it is obviously all too easy to fall, unlike many versions where the reader must wonder how anyone could fall down such a tiny mound. Tom, the piper's son, is seen running away down the page-length street. The illustration for 'Moses supposes his toeses are roses', the essence of the sounds being O, is itself circular and all its contents are round and O-like also. The decision to use black and white for some rhymes and colour for others was appropriate in each case and the whole work forms a satisfying visual experience justifying the Kate Greenaway Award it received.

Nursery rhymes are passed on orally from generation to generation and each generation sees a new crop of nursery rhyme books, either collection of rhymes as in the Opie and Briggs and Blakeley volumes mentioned earlier or the versions of simple rhymes, as in for example, Maureen Roffey's *Tinker Tailor Soldier Sailor*.

The next stage of picture book tends to be the counting

and alphabet books, most of which are not systematic attempts to instil numeracy and literacy, but attitude-formation books which by the use of colour and objects make a start on the process of recognizing letters and numbers. Many fail to provide the clarity of illustration, the familiarity of objects and the repetition needed to lodge in the memory, but some of these can be looked at as picture books rather than as alphabet or counting books, and Brian Wildsmith's *ABC* is the classic example, where strong colours of page and of painting provide a feast for the eyes, making of secondary importance the fact that some of the objects are likely to be unknown to most children as in the 'I for Iguana'.

The large number of counting books makes it necessary for adults intending to use them with children to distinguish between those which facilitate learning to count and those which are picture books on the theme of number. In the latter category, is William Stobb's *A Widemouthed Gaping Waddling Frog*, which may be typical Stobbs painting but which does not in either text or illustrations aid counting. In the former category is Alex Brychta's *Numbers One to Ten and Back Again* where even the title indicates the necessary repetition and where the illustrations are clear, and relevant to every child who lives where there are buses, and where, in humorous style, the text is simple and re-inforcing.

Still with a mild 'educative' purpose are those picture books where each page has one object or scene designed to promote identification, recognition and information. These vary from, for instance, the Methuen *Look and See* books which show familiar everyday activities in one photograph per page; such as *Bathtime*; or Dean Hay's books with clear colour page design and photographs of, for example, *Things in the Kitchen*, or the Bodley Head board books with one simple colour illustration per page.

These are related to the beautifully simple yet rich books

by Dick Bruna, where the clear outline, chunky figures and objects are attractive, non-distracting and informative, as in his *My Vest is White*.

More detailed pictures are enjoyed by the young child for browsing and pointing out and in some cases for the humour, for example Peter Spier's books, or in different style the Richard Scarry books, and differently humorous again, the Dr Seuss books and Arnold Lobel's *Frog and Toad*.

The vast majority of children's picture books tell a story in pictures with words that may take up only two or three lines to a page. There is no one style that can identify such a book for a particular age or interest market, the range is enormous. It covers Maurice Sendak's unique style of thought and illustration in his own *Where the Wild Things Are* and *In the Night Kitchen* or in his illustrations for Janice M. Udry's *The Moon Jumpers*; Charles Keeping's strong illustration in his many books, e.g. *Joseph's Yard*; Ezra Jack Keats' particular collage style in *Snowy Day* and *Peter's Chair*; the distinctive style and colouring in the work of the Japanese artists such as Mitsumasa Anno in *The King's Flower* and his extraordinary *Anno's Alphabet*, or Satomi Ichikawa's *From Morn to Midnight* and *The Friends*. It covers the black and white illustrative style of Wanda Gag used in *Millions of Cats*, the puppet features of Jiri Trnka's work, the water colours of Edward Ardizzone, the clarity of line in the work of Robert McCluskey and Pat Hutchins, the warmth and comfort of Shirley Hughes' work, the cartoon style of William Papas and the baroque style of Errol le Cain.

There are hundreds of illustrators throughout the world producing picture books of fine quality and a glance at the Kate Greenaway, Caldecott and Hans Andersen Award lists will indicate the range of styles and nationalities. There is also in some countries, a vast quantity of mass market picture books with trite storyline, garish pictures and ready availability in stores and supermarkets. To some extent this has been counteracted by the availability over the last ten years of paperback editions of quality picture books, usually photo-reduced from the originals.

In some countries government publishing houses and educational bodies are as yet the only producers of picture books, and these tend to be to a formula of cheap, paper-covered, unimaginative, 'educational' content, largely because there are insufficient funds for better quality production and because there is not a pool of children's book illustrators and designers.

At the present time there is a gulf between that kind of publication and the inspired artistic works of many children's book illustrators in a free market. There is also a difference in price, as many Western publishers are finding in their efforts to keep down the costs of full colour quality illustration in hard cover.

There are thousands of picture books that tell a story for the child who is not yet competent in reading a longer text, but it is important to recognize that the picture book is a work in its own right not necessarily aimed only at the young child. There is a common belief that the picture book is for young children who cannot read and is thus to be ignored once the child can read. This belief is perpetuated by many teachers who denounce a child who can read, if he chooses to look at a picture book. Similarly librarians who shelve picture books only in kinder-boxes or under labels such as 'for the young child' are doing a disservice to many illustrators and to many children.

There may be a tendency for older children to simply glance at the pictures on the page, that is, to *see* them rather than *look* at them, looking involving a more positive, active, conscious approach. When a picture does not engage attention in this way the illustrator has failed at a deep level though the level of surface information and pleasure may be achieved.

103

Some picture book illustrators purposely pay attention to a conscious process of looking, for example Anthony Browne's *A Walk in the Park* and *Through the Magic Mirror* depict at first glance ordinary scenes but the eye that is looking soon catches the incongruous and each page becomes an exercise in spotting the oddity – a tree trunk like a leg, a park seat with shoes, an eggcup in a bird's nest.

The graphic brilliance of Mitsumasa *Anno's Alphabet* similarly attracts close inspection of perspective, and there are many picture books in which the reader is specifically invited to spot the objects or consequences.

There is a distinction to be made between the picture book that is concerned with things obviously related to the very young child and the book of pictures and text which speaks to older children and even teenagers and adults. Examples include Fiona French's *Aio the Rainmaker*, which has an African tribal flavour in text and illustration and which has more appeal to a readership of age 8 to adult than to a small child; Michael Foreman's *All the King's Horses* which begins:

> In distant time, on the far-off plateaus of Asia,
> lived a princess. She wasn't the milk-white,
> golden-haired pink little number the way princes-
> ses are supposed to be. This was a BIG girl. And
> dark.

The title refers to the large number of horses acquired by the King as forfeits from all the suitors who failed to beat the princess in wrestling bouts. The big princess is shown tying all the men in knots, the epitome of what the author/illustrator is doing to the traditional fairy tale theme, women's place in society and conventional female romantic aspirations; blatantly sexist in reverse, with a dominant female.

A similarly adult parable is Russell Hoban's *The Dancing*

Tigers, illustrated by David Gentleman, and gently mocking modern society.

In this category of picture books for older children and adults are books using picture strip style, such as Herge's *Tintin* books, Goscinny and Uderzo's *Asterix* books and Raymond Briggs' *Fungus The Bogeyman*, each of which has adult characters, clever vocabulary and sentence structure and illustrative detail. Though the three illustrators have totally different styles each is master of the picture strip format as an art form and each offers levels of interest, irony and enjoyment to a very wide age range.

There are few specific characteristics of a picture book in that, as in story books, the picture book themes cover fairy, folk and fantasy, animals real and imaginary, social situations in home, school, environment, human relationships within the family and without.

The illustrators use vastly differing methods of illustration ranging from black and white, through pastel shades to strong primary colours to glorious technicolour using pencil, water-colour, oils, collage, chalk, scraperboard and a variety of other materials and techniques.

Most picture books are sixteen or thirty-two pages in length and most are, by tradition, intended for the age group that has not yet begun to read any length of text. But increasingly, there are themes and styles that appeal to older children and young adults, and some that are more for collectors than for children.

Children's books with illustrations
The distinction here is that picture books have more illustration than text whereas the illustrated children's book is text accompanied by either line drawings at intervals throughout the book, or as page decoration, or chapter headings or tailpieces, or the occasional colour illustration.

Many surveys show that older children prefer to have little or no illustration in their storybooks other than the cover design. It seems that pictures interfere with the mental image of the character or scene and in some cases indicate an age of character which does not conform to the age of the reader and is therefore possibly an unconscious deterrant to reading the book. This does not apply to books for the child who is just beginning the transfer from picture book to full length story book and most publishers providing books for that age group include illustrations both to give clues to the text and to break up the slabs of print.

Some of the classic story books whether popular or esoteric are remembered for the way in which the illustrations complement and extend the story, as in Shepard's pictures for *Winnie the Pooh* or Tenniel's *Alice in Wonderland*, or Mabel Lucy Attwell's for *The Water Babies*; the illustrations for Richmal Crompton's *William* books and those for Enid Blyton's *Famous Five* books, and the pictures in *The Hardy Boys* all contribute to the overall impression of the books in children's minds.

But the great majority of children's books with illustrative content go unremarked, despite the naming of the illustrator or decorator on the title page. The exceptions are notable, as in Ann Strugnell's art work in *North American Legends* edited by Virginia Haviland, or Charles Keeping's explosive illustrations in *God Beneath the Sea* by Edward Blishen and Leon Garfield, or Pauline Baynes' numerous works, including her illustrations for the award winning *Dictionary of Chivalry*. The illustration of non-fiction books is discussed in both the section on information books and the section on selection and evaluation.

Books with unusual physical features
There are available many unusual books for children, unusual in that visual or tactile means are used in addition to

106

print and picture. The following list indicates the nature of such books:

Board books
Concertina
Rag books
Flap
Half page
Cut out
Pop-up
Scratch and sniff
Overlays and mirror
Noise books
Touch and tell
Braille

Although few can be considered children's literature by literary criteria there are several purposes behind their publication which make them useful, valuable and enjoyable to children. The over-riding purpose is to facilitate communication and as the child may need to use all his senses with these books, such use is an aid to comprehension.

For instance board books, those with stiff card backs and pages, are useful for the young, or handicapped child who has difficulty in turning a normal page, and who may otherwise cause excessive wear and tear. The Bodley Head Board Books with rounded corners and simple, colourful content, are good examples. Rag or cloth books are often concerned with popular characters such as Walt Disney's, but may fill a need in young and handicapped children. Similarly concertina books which unfold to a long strip, are of variable quality, the best unfolding to form excellent wall friezes.

The use of flaps and half pages enables some writers and illustrators to provide an extra stimulation to the imagination as in John Goodall's books without words, which employ the device of a half page flap to extend the action and the scene, or Helen Oxenbury's series *Heads, Bodies and Legs*, in which each book's nine pages are divided into three strips of board within a spiral binding, so that the child can create ludicrous combinations of people or animals. Another example is that of a simple book, *Where's Spot?* by Eric Hill, a do-it-yourself book about a disappearing puppy. It involves reading the large print question on each page and opening the door in the picture, lifting the piano lid, the bed flounce, the rug, to see if Spot is there. It is effective in its page engineering, the children can actually 'open' and 'lift' and the story itself has suspense, action and a happy ending.

Visual features abound in pop-up books which can vary from poor quality to the award-winning *Haunted House* by Jan Pienkowski. Everything associated with haunted houses is contained within boxes that literally creak, cupboards that open, eyes that move. Those things that cannot be contained spring out at the reader; a spider from the hall ceiling, an octopus from the kitchen sink, a gorilla from the depths of an armchair and a bat from the attic. Odd things happen under the lavatory seat and behind the bed panelling. Pulling the arrow tabs and simply opening the pages cause 'things' to appear. Pienkowski's story and pictures are put into this form, called paper engineering, by Tor Lokvig.

Pictures that stand up on a page have an attraction far beyond the actual content of the picture, as have the books that use overlays and mirrors to create changing visual effects.

There are books which offer sounds also, as in the 'Noise' books, in which a squeak or other sound is achieved by pressing the page, or in the books containing a record or disc of words or music related to the text.

The sense of smell is employed when reading the 'scratch and sniff' or 'sniff and tell' books, in which a relevant odour is incorporated in micro-dots in a picture. When scratched the fragrance is released and therefore adds further information for the reader.

The most recent innovation is in the books for the blind and partially sighted, whereby a story is told in printed text and in braille, with raised surface pictures for the child to 'feel'. 'Touch and tell' or 'twin-vision' books are exemplified by Virginia Allen Jensen and Dorcas Woodbury Haller's *What's That?* in which shapes and concepts are 'felt' in embossed pictures as part of the story told in print and braille.

Touch is also used in the books where the pages have tactile objects in them or on them. The former is exemplified by Methuen's books *Wheels Go Round* and *One Green Frog*, where laminated holes go right through the pages in diminishing sizes. Books with things to be touched are often made individually and there is in Japan an organization called the Co-ordinating Committee for the Promotion of Cloth Picture Books, which is concerned with handmade books in which various materials, such as leather, paper, wool, beads, plastic, fur and bark are used for the child to feel. Intended mainly for handicapped children they have also found a ready interest amongst non-handicapped children in the Tokyo Public Libraries.

The availability of 'toy' books and books of unusual format provides another means of comprehension, learning and enjoyment for many children.

Illustration in children's books uses most of the methods available to artists, particularly in the picture book format. As the child progresses to short story and then full-length novel for children the amount of illustration is reduced in quantity and changes from full colour to black and white line drawings. By the time the reader has reached the adult book he will be dependent upon the power of the printed word to evoke mental images.

But the visual image in fiction and information book is a necessary part of reading in most stages of growth to mature readers. It provides information, confirmation, aesthetic pleasure and emotional satisfaction, if the artist has perceived the relationship between the theme and the child.

Further readings

Alderson, Brian. *Looking at Picture Books*. London, National Book League, 1974

Cianciolo, Patricia J. *Picture Books for Children*. Chicago, A.L.A., 2nd. ed. 1980

Hurlimann, Bettina. *Picture Book World*. London, O.U.P., 1967

Miller, Bertha M. and others. *Illustrators of Children's Books* 1744–1945, 1946–1958, 1957–1966. Boston, Hornbook, 1947, 1968 and 1977.

Moss, Elaine. Series of articles on illustrators *in Signal* e.g. Shirley Hughes in *Signal*, May 1980

Watts, Lynne and Nisbet, John. *Legibility in Children's Books*. London, N.F.E.R. 1974

CHAPTER SEVEN

The Reading Needs and Interests of Children

Having spent some time on what children's literature is I can now look at who needs it and why. Books do not exist in a vacuum, they are made to be read.

I have already indicated that individual people have individual preferences in books though there may be books which children *must* read for school or examination purposes. The development of critical faculties and personal taste are part of the whole reading process and just as we have likes and dislikes in our food so we have taste and distaste in our reading, whether child or adult. This can be called 'reading-interests', that is, those books or themes which interest children. But interest is not necessarily the same as need.

There are at least three categories of 'need' in relationship to books. A child may 'need' a book in order to get information for a specific school essay or project or in order to find out about a hobby, 'need' here meaning actual physical access to the required book. The second area of 'need' is more likely to be subconscious and refers to what happens to the mind of the reader when he is reading. This kind of need is usually recognized by the adult responsible for children's reading and results in broad statements like, 'Young children "need" a happy ending to their stories because they are not sufficiently mature to cope with unhappy endings'; 'Because each Western teenager tends to think that he or she is alone in the suffering or distress facing

111

him, teenagers "need" books which enable them to see, firstly, that others have been there before them, and secondly, that the problem or distress was resolved, or at least coped with, if only in the way shown in the story.'

I can also make broad statements about a third category of 'need'. That is the 'need' which adults impose or require to be satisfied, as in 'children "need" books which are well written so that they are introduced to good language and sentence structure'. Or 'children "need" books which present them with an acceptable view of their country/moral issue/ death/sex/politics/religion/adults', acceptable in terms of the school or the parents or the State. Or 'children who are slow learners "need" books with simplified language and lots of pictures'.

The difference between these three areas of reading 'need' and that of reading 'interest' can be shown in a child's simple statement, I like books about . . . In other words, he is interested in . . . .

Now there is a wealth of analytical discussion on what reading is for, and what happens to the mind as a result of reading fiction. The reading list at the end of the book recommends some books which will lead you further on this aspect, but basically there is often a link between the second kind of 'need' and reading 'interest'. A child may show a preference for, a taste for, an interest in, certain kinds of book *because* they satisfy a subconscious or unconscious need in him. There are obviously too many such links to categorize but when a child says, 'That was a good book!', we know that some need in him was satisfied and that he is likely to be interested then in more of the same.

This feeling is sometimes called *therapeutic* in the sense that it has a curative power, or *cathartic*, meaning cleansing or purifying. Over a short period of time there has developed the science of bibliotherapy, which is the practice of using certain books or stories as part of the treatment of children and adults who are emotionally or mentally disturbed.

Trained bibliotherapists can sometimes help such people to come to terms with their problems through reading stories which have a relevance to their problems. In much less dramatic ways most children and adults who can read sufficiently well or who can listen to stories, receive this satisfying and constructive feeling with the 'right' stories. Children and adults who can read continue to do so, voluntarily, because they enjoy it. This enjoyment comes from:

1. Seeing oneself vicariously in fictional form
2. Taking on another's character in dream or wish fulfilment
3. Showing how others tackled situations/problems, good and bad
4. The information obtained.

Many other benefits occur in the reading process and these are indicated in Chapter Ten.

There is obviously a strong connection between what children want and need in books and the criteria for selecting by librarians and teachers, although reading can mean different things to different people depending upon the reason for which the reading is being undertaken. Reading for pleasure, reading to pass the time, reading for the imaginative experience, reading to obtain information, reading to practice the skill of reading, all these and more mean that a multiplicity of books and kinds of book is needed, from reading schemes for learning to read, through comics and periodicals, to story books and information books.

There are, in some countries, books for all kinds of reading and reader, from those catering for the relaxed pleasant time of a good reader, to what is often a hard demanding time for the poor reader.

During the years that I worked in three quite different

countries, a highly developed country, a developing country and a very undeveloped country, I discovered that whatever a child reads, voluntarily, can be helpful to him, despite the belief amongst some children's literature specialists and some teachers, that only 'good' children's literature should be made available to children and young people. But that aspect is looked at in more detail in the chapter on selection criteria.

Often what children choose to read is a clue to their emotional, educational and intellectual stage, and librarians, teachers and parents should use those clues when attempting to bring children and books together. The detailed criteria for selecting books to fit children's needs and interests are given in Chapter Eight but what follows here is an outline of interests expressed by children, as shown in surveys of children's reading interests, local, national, large and small.

Factors affecting children's reading interests
1. The existence of a range of published books
2. The availability of children's books in the home, the school, the library, the bookshop
3. The selection made by adults (teachers, librarians, booksellers, parents) on behalf of children
4. Time and opportunity to read
5. Children's own personal needs and abilities

These are all factors to note when studying published surveys of children's reading interests and habits, or when undertaking such surveys. In many countries individual librarians or teachers attempt to find out which books and categories of reading interest children. In some countries large-scale surveys are undertaken to assess national or regional readership and compare possible geographical, sex, age, social status or ability differences. The possibilities are endless and there is a danger of drawing false conclusions if the sample and the methodology are not carefully devised to take account of these factors.

When applied to statistical surveys such factors are called variables, meaning that the findings or significance of the findings may vary according to age, sex, ability, origin of the children and these must be taken into account in the planning stage of the survey.

In Britain and USA most of the surveys, whether national or local, show children's broad preferences for certain kinds of book at certain stages and ages.

Children's reading preferences

Beginning in early childhood there is a preference for books that allow the child to participate while the parent or other person is reading aloud. For instance nursery rhymes, folk rhymes, simple fairy stories, song books, finger-play or action books, simple picture books with stories set in everyday life, tales concerned with animals or toys, all please the child because he can make noises, do the actions, point to the objects and characters in the pictures and repeat the words read aloud. The basic reason for this preference is not only the actual book, but also the fact that at that age the child is *sharing* the book with an adult or older child and the book is a stimulus to communication and a means of enjoying the attention of the person who is reading to him. In the section on illustration more detail is given on picture books for the young but here the concern is with the child's preference rather than the adult's assessment of what is needed or useful.

The next stage in most countries is from ages five to eight when children are just learning to read, may not yet be capable of reading a full length children's book and prefer books with pictures partly because they can give a clue to the text and partly from the sheer enjoyment of the visual story. At this stage too there is a preference for fairy and folk tales in various forms, some in picture book form, some in illustrated re-tellings and some in collections of tales. This choice develops from the oral tradition and in some countries where there is little published material, there still exists the tradition of family and community storytelling for all age groups. Books of folk and fairy tales are a link between what is already known orally and the same thing in printed form, thus providing familiarity. As with all reading, familiarity with the subject content makes the reading easier and more comprehensible.

At this age also there is generally an interest in animal stories, both real and humanized, reflecting the fact that many children develop a strong feeling for their pet animals and their toy animals and project on to these their own joys and frustrations.

Adventure stories too feature high on the list of preferences at the top end of this age range and continuing into the next period, the nine to thirteen group. It is in this middle period of childhood that many children find pleasure in the stories of children having adventures without their parents, solving mysteries, catching criminals, overcoming difficulties, coping in an adult world; books which liberate the children's own feelings of being restricted by parental and authority's control. Such wishful thinking on the part of children is one of the reasons why there is such immense interest in series such as the American Hardy Boys and the Bobbsey Twins and in Britain's Enid Blyton books featuring the Famous Five and the Secret Seven, all of which are still read eagerly by thousands of children all over the world regardless of age or ability.

Other countries have their examples of popular adventure series for both boys and girls and most countries have produced individual titles which show children meeting challenges, getting into difficulties, achieving success or glory and, usually, returning to the safety of home and family at the end.

In many countries children in the eight to thirteen range are already showing the distinct difference between boys' and girls' reading preferences. At this age girls are interested in school stories, horse stories, animals, works of fantasy and imagination, historical stories and nature books, while the boys prefer adventure stories, funny books and have a strong and growing preference for non-fiction in the form of books on technical and scientific subjects and hobbies such as sports, birds and stamp collecting. In the fourteen plus age range young people in many countries read less than ever and boys read less than girls. When boys do read they read considerably more non-fiction than fiction, whereas girls read more fiction than non-fiction.

There are many countries where young people of fourteen have finished school education and will not have achieved a level of literacy that enables them to read fluently enough to enjoy books. But in those countries where teenagers can read and do have books available to them, the preferences amongst the girls are first, romantic books, then humorous stories followed by historical novels and ghost stories, while teenage boys prefer humorous books, adventure (mostly adult adventure fiction), mystery, war books and science fiction.

Children want or need information books for:

1. Individual interest, at home and at school
2. Reference – finding specific information
3. Project or schoolwork

When children read non-fiction they want information in terms of facts, concepts or attitudes and they need an understanding of that information in the context of the *purpose* for which they are reading the book. Many of the more successful information books are those which attempt to place the information in the reader's context, subtly.

Facts on their own can be useful and these tend to be

117

found in the quick-reference books like dictionaries, direc-tories, and encyclopaedias, but the important aspect of read-ing information books lies not only in the information gained but in the thought processes involved in understanding the information and then in making use of it. More detail is given in the section on book selection and in the section on information books. In the non-fiction fields the preferences are for the natural sciences (animals, birds, biology), practi-cal subjects, geographical and historical books, social science themes, arts and crafts and sex.

Within each of the fiction themes there is wide variation in quality amongst the books read. Describing children's read-ing preferences for subject matter does not imply that they read only quality books in these subjects and one of the aims of teachers and librarians, in countries where children and young people are literate, and have a choice of reading mat-erials, is to lead the reader to the well-written book on the preferred theme.

In all the surveys of reading interests the difference be-tween those of boys and those of girls is striking, even in countries where there are attempts to change sex discrimina-tion in the ways children are reared. There are some factors which may influence the differences: biological, family up-bringing, social conditioning, educational requirements; but there is not yet a clear reason for the different reading pre-ferences. It is also noticeable that in many countries the boys who do read voluntarily at fourteen plus (and in some cases at twelve plus) are interested in *adult* adventure, mystery and science fiction books, and that large numbers of teenage girls from twelve plus read large quantities of adult romantic and historical fiction.

Physical aspects of the book
In addition to interest in subject themes, both fictional and non-fictional, there are preferences for physical aspects of

118

the book. Surveys indicate that from the age of about twelve young people show a clear preference for the paperback or pocketbook edition of a book, rather than the hardback. This is likely to be the result of a number of factors:

1. Cover (or jacket) attraction: the cover of a paperback is usually different from that of the hardback edition and is designed to appeal to the mass market and casual buyer.
2. The size: this makes it look less daunting, easier to read in terms of apparent length, and easier to handle for carrying in bag or pocket.
3. Appearance: it does not look like a school book and is therefore psychologically more likely to be enjoyable.
4. Cost: it is cheaper than a hardback edition and therefore it is possible for the reader to enjoy the pleasure of ownership.
5. Availability: it is more likely to be found in newsagents, stores, supermarkets, market stalls, bookshops and school bookclubs; in other words, paperbacks tend to be where people are.

Given a choice, other physical factors for which most children show preference in books are the external appearance, the presence of illustrations, well laid out text and reasonable print size.

It has been noted in many countries that when children select books from the shelves they look first at the title and if it is intriguing enough they take the book off the shelf, glance at the cover of the book, flick through the pages to see how difficult the text looks in terms of legibility and in difficulty of vocabulary; look at some of the illustrations if there are any; read the 'blurb' to see what the book is about; and then either select or reject it.

This is not so for paperback selection by teenagers, preference there being for interesting cover, intriguing title, narrative style, set in contemporary times, high on physical action and with one main character.

Adults' reading needs in children's literature

Parents, teachers and librarians also need or want children's books and have reading preferences within children's literature. They want or need children's books for use with children:

1. To entertain
2. To increase knowledge
3. To encourage individual learning and use of books.

When parents select books for their children or offer guidance they tend to have two main preferences, to find and share with the child the books of their own youth, which may or may not be relevant to the age, experience, social circumstances or ability of the child, and to provide the child with books that they think will develop him, usually in the 'educational' sense. In some cases parents are seduced by the visual attractions of the cover or the illustrations.

Teachers need books which will complement and supplement their teaching, whether fictional or subject based themes. They want and prefer children's books which do this clearly, in accordance with whatever standards obtain in their school or teaching field and which fit the particular age and ability of their students, in school matters. Some teachers see that the child is a child first and a school pupil second, and want *for* the child books that have something to say to the whole child.

Librarians' needs and interests in children's literature are much more widespread and varied. What the librarian needs is physical access to stock appropriate for the library's clientele. Most children's librarians are professionally interested in children's literature as a broad genre of writing, the literary, psychological, educational and sociological factors, and most have a personal interest in one or other kind of book for children.

Many other adults in a community or a nation have needs and interests in children's books, either from a literary standpoint or because they are involved with children and need to know something about the relationship of books to children.

Children's reading interests can be ascertained by means of surveys, questionnaires, observation and simply by asking them. But it is important to bear in mind that a need may be for a book that a child ought to have for his work that would enable him to do a better project or essay and to learn more, *or*, unidentified by the child but recognized by an adult as necessary for the child. A want can be described as what the reader would like to have; evidence of a desire or an interest; and a demand is what a reader asks for. So librarians and teachers concerned with providing books should be aware that children may demand, or ask for, books that they do not need and need books that they do not want or ask for.

It makes good sense for anyone involved in promoting books to children, for whatever purpose, to try to obtain some indication of interest and need in order to better carry out the task of evaluating and selecting books for children.

Further readings

Kujoth, Jean Spealman. *Reading Interests of Children and Young Adults*. Metuchen, Scarecrow, 1970

Marshall, Margaret R. *Libraries and Literature for Teenagers*. London, Deutsch, 1975

Meek, Margaret ed. *The Cool Web; the pattern of children's reading*. London, Bodley Head, 1977

Whitehead, Frank and others. *Children and Their Books*. Schools Council Project. London, Macmillan, 1977

CHAPTER EIGHT

Evaluation and Selection of Children's Books

Evaluation and selection pre-suppose:

1. An objective or a purpose for which the selection is to be made.
2. Criteria or standards by which the material is to be evaluated.
3. Sufficient quantity of material from which to make a selection or with which to make a comparison, though selection is of course involved in a choice between only two items.
4. A selector or evaluator.
5. Actual and potential user.

Any individual, whether child or adult, exercises his critical faculties, his judgement, his preferences when 'choosing' a book. Though such judgement or preference may be unspoken, unwritten, illogical or unconscious, it is nevertheless the result of a known need, or of experience, or of the subconscious.

But when the selector is selecting for others much more conscious judgement, assessment and objectives are brought into play. Still more factors are involved when the selector is selecting for children, as indicated in the chapter on children's reading needs and interests. Often there is an element of the selectors's own didacticism when selecting books to be read by children, a didacticism which may be bad or good depending upon the restrictive or liberal nature of the aims.

When librarians and teachers select children's books for libraries or classes they are working from an often unquestioned assumption that reading books is a 'good thing', without necessarily having formulated exactly what the good effects are. However, there are many librarians and educators and students who have given thought to these broad objectives. I required students of librarianship, teachers and teacher-librarians studying children's literature to discuss what they thought reading did to and for children and to compile a list of broad objectives for the provision of books for children. Some of the results were the same as those published in articles and policy statements in various countries and the following are examples culled from many sources. The list can be used as broad policy for the provision of books for children, bearing in mind that the examples given spring from the laudable desire of the selectors to educate/develop/stretch/enrich the minds of child readers and from their conviction that books exist which will achieve this aim. In many countries the dearth of children's books, or their poor quality, present teachers and librarians with little opportunity for selection. Whatever is obtainable is needed. But in such countries, and in those where there is a wide range of children's literature, the following, which is not in any order of priority, may be a helpful basis when selecting books for children.

Select books that:

1. Reflect national, local and individual values, experiences and scenes.
2. Introduce children to their own cultural heritage.
3. Provide a vicarious experience of a world they do not live in, in terms of time, space and culture.
4. Enlarge the mind and the imagination.
5. Offer experience in the creative and scientific inquiry process.

6. Enable the reader to acquire, or change, knowledge, values and attitudes.
7. Encourage an appreciation of beauty and human achievement, motivation and aspiration.
8. Allow the discernment of good/bad, right/wrong.
9. Contribute towards development intellectually, psychologically and socially.
10. Provide enjoyment.

T. S. Eliot in his *Notes Towards the Definition of Culture* said that there were three permanent reasons for reading, 'the acquisition of wisdom, the enjoyment of art and the pleasure of entertainment'; a neat summary of the list above.

To these broad aims can be added more specific aims depending upon the circumstances in which selection is taking place. For example there could be requirements such as:

1. Motivate retarded/remedial children to read.
2. Present fantasy and fact pictorially.
3. Complement and supplement the teaching in the school.
4. Provide material for storytelling.
5. Offer information for a project.
6. Enable parents to share books with their pre-school child.

Again, these are still quite broad aims, based largely on the known needs of the children or organization or library for which the selector is selecting. Within each of these examples it is possible to specify in great detail the criteria to be applied in order to achieve those ends, criteria for both fiction and non-fiction.

However in this book, intended to introduce aspects of the very wide subject of children's literature, it is necessary only to touch on the kinds of criteria used in evaluation and selection.

For instance in the selection and evaluation of fiction

there is the evaluation applied in terms of for whom the work is being considered, its place in the total library or collection, its format and price, and there is the much more difficult set of criteria related to the literary content.

This aspect is of course paramount when books are being selected for literary awards or studied in literature classes. The same kinds of literary analysis can be applied to children's literature as to any literature and further readings on this are given at the end of the chapter. Bearing in mind that the experience of literature by the evaluator provides a basis for comparison and helps towards the development of an almost intuitive 'feel' for recognizing what is good, consideration should be given to the following aspects when attempting the literary evaluation of a children's book.

Fiction
1. The subject matter ought to have been chosen by the writer because he has something to say on the theme, something that is original. Although the theme may be commonplace the author's, or his characters', view must be original, stretching the imagination and widening knowledge.
2. The action should carry out the idea, with events and characters progressing, not necessarily logically, but acceptably within the limits set by the theme. There should be no recourse to outside agencies hitherto unrelated to the plot, no solving the problem or alleviating the situation by unrelated intervention.
3. The characters should 'live'. Their strengths, weaknesses, credibility, conviction, inter-relation must flow from the picture built up through the narration, conversation, thoughts of others and individual actions, which all contribute to a convincing and integrated portrait of a character.
4. A sense of time and environment should form the basis

whether the story is set in the past, present or future.

5. Language, vocabulary, sentence structure make up the components of what is often called style. The style of writing may vary from one book to another, though written by the same author, if he considers that the style is a necessary part of the total impact of the theme. But usually there are individual clues, idiosyncrasies, patterns of thought or of words which can identify the great writers, the prolific writers and the formula writers. Aspects of style include factors such as how appropriate the language use is to the subject matter; the balance of narration and dialogue; natural dialogue, sentence patterns; mood creation, e.g. mystery, gloom, evil, joy, security.

An essential factor also is the style of illustration and its relevance to the theme of the book, complementing and supplementing and extending the writing style.

6. A sense of reality, even in fantasy, makes for a good book, in that there is pleasure not merely from the surface enjoyment of a good read, but the deeper if subconscious, satisfaction of having gone through a vicarious, but at the time of reading, *real* experience.

7. The literary value lies not so much in the subject or theme as in how that theme is presented, how it is revealed to the child reader's perceptions.

Literary analysis starts then with asking questions such as: What did the author intend to do? How did he attempt it? Did he achieve it? If not, why not?

Other forms of analysis and evaluation can start from different bases as indicated earlier in the chapter, though all must be taken into account when selecting books for children.

Non-fiction
Selecting non-fiction for effective reading means taking into

126

account:

1. The purpose for which it is being read.
2. Recognition of the kinds of non-fiction which will facilitate that purpose.
3. Availability of non-fiction works suitable for effecting that purpose.
4. Awareness of the physical features of non-fiction which aid effective reading.
5. Ensuring that the skills needed for effective use are learned by the children so that they *can* read effectively what you and they have selected.

There are at least two basic aspects to note when selecting non-fiction or information books; first the detailed features applicable to any information book and then the potential use to which the specific book can be put.

Criteria for the first aspect can be described under the following headings:

1. Content:
   a. Scope, broad or specific; starting and finishing at what level of knowledge or at what points in the subject matter.
   b. Accuracy of factual information and illustrative content; evidence of generalizations or bias; up-to-dateness of the information.
2. Authority:
   Related to the above, authority can be assessed by noting the author's experience, qualifications or other credentials in the subject field; by the reputation of the series and/or publisher.
3. Presentation:
   a. Style appropriate to the subject and to intended use in terms of language e.g. technical, simple, popular, descriptive, discursive.
   b. Appropriate to age in the concepts offered; the lay-

out; the kinds of illustration; the arrangement or organization of the information in terms of chronological, A–Z etc.

c. Use of chapters, headings, references, diagrams, maps, etc.

d. Use of primary sources where appropriate.

e. Presence of helpful features like contents list, pagination, glossary, further reading list (of books suitable for a similar age/level of reader), index.

4. Illustration:

a. The importance of visual information, preferably in colour.

b. Relevant to the text.

c. Positioning in the text.

d. Style of illustration e.g. representational, abstract, photographic, original source pictorial material, decorative rather than informative.

5. Format:

a. Size, in terms of handling by intended readership; psychological appeal; wear and tear.

b. Binding suitable for intended use.

c. Quality of paper to ensure clarity, appeal and use.

d. Print; legibility, clarity, distinction between headings; use of italics or bold type for emphasis; avoidance of slabs of print by use of margins, indenting, headings, white space etc.

6. Assessment of overall quality in its own right as a readable, comprehensible and informative book, and then in comparison with other works on the same topic.

There are selection criteria and evaluation criteria in addition to these general aspects, special criteria applicable to particular subject fields such as science or to particular kinds of reference work such as encyclopaedias or dictionaries. There are also the possibilities in some countries that questions are asked about information books which appear to violate required principles concerning racism, sexism, violence, political or religious stances.

However, coverage of the first aspect, concerned with the book inside and outside, must now lead into the second aspect, that of considering potential usage.

Potential usage
Potential usage of a non-fiction work brings up the need to assess the book for its potential to answer the kinds of questions that might be put to it. This is related to the scope and presentation of the content and to the author's style of writing.

Certain kinds of information need require certain kinds of information book and, on the part of the reader, particular forms of reading skill or strategy.

An information book can be a fact book capable of providing nuggets of information in answer to specific queries such as: What were the dates of the Battle of Gettysburg, the independence of Nigeria, the first Russian spaceship, Captain Cook's landing in Australia, the end of the Second World War?; or, How many legs has a spider? What are the colours of the rainbow? What is the chemical symbol for water? All these are straightforward facts requiring the reader simply to locate them in the information book and identify them as the answer to his question. He would therefore select the kind of information book that facilitated quick answers to these quick questions.

But his question may be more complex and require an information book capable of providing that further information to questions like; What caused the Battle of Gettysburg? or, How do spiders make webs?, to which there are answers that are relatively non-controversial but more detailed than the previous answers. These would require a more detailed book in which the reader locates the information, identifies it as basically appropriate, sorts it mentally and selects the aspects which together give the answer.

Still more complex questions can be asked of an information book and a much more complex reading strategy may be required of the reader in finding the answers to questions like; What were the effects of the Battle of Gettysburg compared with those of Custer's Last Stand? or, What is the role of the spider in the world of nature? Here the reader must select a book which goes much more deeply and analytically into the subject matter, and in addition to locating the information and identifying it as basically applicable, the reader must then assimilate the information, analyse it, compare it and contrast it, and *understand* it, before being able to answer the question, because there are few books which provide all sides of every subject. The onus is often on the reader to make the connection.

Thus the selector may need to ask, in the knowledge of the readers for whom the selection is made, is this book capable of answering one or more of the types of question my readers will put to it? Can this book provide the answers better pictorially via the illustrations and other visual aids in the book than by the text? Pictures can be a visual language, more informative than text, but the two together, if well-designed, can be of maximum aid to children and young people who have a reading problem.

Selecting for the reading-retarded child
Much more detail is given on this aspect of selection in my books *Libraries and Literature for Teenagers* and *Libraries and the Handicapped Child*, but here the basic problems and criteria for selection can be outlined.

The causes of reading retardation can be tabulated as:

1. Mental inability.
2. Gender – more boys than girls have a reading problems.

130

3. Social factors.
4. Language problems.
5. Handicaps, e.g. hearing impairment, visual impairment, physical.
6. Emotional problems and maladjustment.
7. Poor teaching.

The less able reader, or backward, retarded, remedial reader but not those we call reluctant, who can read but prefer not to, is found at any age, but the term is generally applied to those who are a year or more behind their contemporaries. They find the familiarity that aids understanding in stories with words that describe what they have experienced or know of, that have relevance to their emotions. The more familiar we are with a situation described the better we understand the text. The easier it becomes to find meaning in what we read the more motivated we shall be to do it again, thus gaining in skill.

Most reading schemes tend to be descriptive rather than analytical in their treatment of the themes concerned and these can be dull. There are now about 150 series published in Britain for the learner reader, with a total of around 2,000 titles. Most are graded reading schemes but some are of sufficient general interest to be stocked in school and public libraries or bought by individuals, and there is an increase in the number of books for the less able teenage reader.

The basic criteria to be applied when selecting books for the reading retarded child can be outlined as follows:

1. Visually attractive material; first of all to gain the attention of the reader so that he will actually pick up the book and open it; then to keep the eye and the mind attracted long enough to enable reading to take place; then to provide interest and pleasure. Daniel Fader in *Hooked on Books* said that 'reading activity follows visual appeal as effect follows cause'.

2. Technically appropriate in vocabulary, sentence length and conceptual content.
3. Physically helpful with clear black print, plenty of white space.
4. Illustrations to aid comprehension. Children use pictures frequently when trying to learn to read, glancing at them for clues to the text.
5. Relevance to the reader's experience, physical or emotional.
6. Humour; this is required to create the positive feeling that despite the efforts required to read, reading can be an enjoyable experience.

But selection can imply rejection, and in school and library terms this is often the practice where there is no agreed upon selection policy, so that what should be positive selection is sometimes a matter of 'choosing' from a range of books by simple elimination.

Rejecting children's books
The reasons for not selecting certain children's books may be threefold, that they do not meet literary, physical or ideological standards or any one or combination of these. A book may be superficial, didactic, with caricatures or stereotyped characters or situations, glamourized, lacking some or all of the criteria discussed earlier or laid down by an award-making body.

Poor physical quality of book production may also necessitate exclusion, depending upon the intended usage or the stated criteria. The price or estimated value for money is often linked with this, though where there is no alternative it is often necessary to select a book despite its poor physical production.

But a common aspect of rejection is that which could be called censorship. This can take the form of pre-censorship, meaning that authors and publishers avoid writing, or publishing, books with a particular theme or content. This varies from country to country depending upon the social/political/ religious mores of the country.

However, even when there is little pre-censorship, books may be rejected by librarians, teachers and parents because the content is thought to be unsuitable. Three reasons are commonly given:

1. To protect the child reader from unpleasant, corrupting or frightening aspects of adult life or of child life.
2. For educational or propagandist purposes in order
   a. to conform to adult requirements/policy from an educational, political or religious viewpoint.
   b. to teach children things that it is thought to be too late to teach adults.
   c. to conform to socio-political rules in countries where there is either a dictator or an ideology which suppresses anything likely to be critical of or in opposition to that ruling power.
3. The child is too young to understand. This is usually applied to subjects such as sex, death, varieties of philosophical, sociological or political opinion or practice.

Censorship is more common in the area of teenage novels than in other kinds of literature for children and young people, the sensitive areas, particularly for USA and Islamic countries, being sex, religion, profanity, violence, drugs and alcohol. But as indicated, 'offensive' passages must be related to their context in the whole work, the reader, whether adult or teenager distinguishing between the pornographic and the lewd treatment, the adolescent ribald vulgarities, and the treatment of sexual relationships as an integral part of the story. Gratuitous violence and its glamourization, and gratuitous profanities, swearing or bad language, would be a cause for concern but the inclusion of violent episodes or of cursing would not of themselves be a reason for rejecting a book.

Crime and violence are enjoyed and coped with by children and teenagers in films, books and magazines. Any suggestion of a co-relation between teenage crime and that kind of reading has been refuted, the high teenage crime rate in many countries being the result of a poor environment, illiteracy and lack of intelligence in most cases.

There are many books in which a 'sensitive' theme is treated responsibly as an integral part of the whole book. Examples include extortion in Robert Cormier's *The Chocolate War*, violence in Bernard Ashley's *Terry on the Fence*, Joan Lingard's *Across the Barricades*, Robert Westall's *The Machine Gunners* and S. E. Hinton's *Rumble Fish*. Drugs are the theme of the latter's *That Was Then This Is Now*. Sex is part of the theme of Judy Blume's *Forever*, Paul Zindel's *My Darling, My Hamburger* and David Rees' *Quentin's Man* and of Aidan Chambers' *Breaktime*. Certain physical functions and unpleasant allusions are found in Raymond Briggs' *Father Christmas* and *Fungus the Bogeyman*, both highly successful in many countries and much appreciated by teenagers almost to the point of cultism.

While many writers find a freedom in writing for teenagers that is not possible when writing for children, most do not abuse that freedom, and most are aware that teenagers today know a great deal about sex, violence, war, racial prejudice, wealth and poverty, from television at a superficial level, or from personal experience. It can be helpful and enjoyable to read a deep exploration of a theme in story form, where the impact of the theme on individuals and society can be felt through characterization and the plot in a serious yet enjoyable treatment.

Then there is rejection of those books with characters or situations which suggest racism or sexism. There is a growing understanding of the ways in which social conditioning affects attitudes both towards people of different sexes and people of differing ethnic backgrounds, and how such attitudes and treatment are reflected in books for children and for adults.

Sexism and racism in books relate to the book's treatment of (usually) women and of people of a race in such a way as to relegate them to secondary or inferior status. This can take the form of always showing girls or women in so-called 'female' occupations and as weak, helpless or evil characters, with boys or men as the main characters, always strong and to be deferred to.

An Indian sociologist, Dr Narendra Nath Kalia, who teaches in the USA, analysed the English language textbooks compiled by the Indian National Council of Educational Research and Training, a federal body. The books, used in most schools in northern India, are written by Indian educationalists and were found to be heavily prejudiced against women, showing them as the 'meek submissive slaves of Indian men' but the NCERT argued that its textbooks reflect Indian social conditions, although it did rewrite some passages in 'progressive' style.

Racism can be identified in books in which white people have power and make decisions regardless of the black or ethnic group in the story; where minority peoples are always presented as a 'problem'; where the effect on the child reader's self image or self esteem is likely to be damaging.

How this should be changed, counterbalanced or censored is a problem which causes heated controversy amongst writers, publishers, librarians, and organizations specifically concerned with abolishing sexist and racist aspects of society, including literature.

The Council on Interracial Books for Children, in New York, and the Writers and Readers Publishing Co-operative, in London, have produced articles and pamphlets on racist and sexist images in children's books, and others have compiled guidelines for non-sexist codes of practice in publishing and in children's book selection. All are concerned with promoting a greater awareness of the way in which society conditions attitudes towards the sexes and towards people of different origins. They are concerned also, not only with encouraging the writing and publishing of books with positive treatment, avoiding discrimination, stereotyping and demeaning characters and situations, but also some are working for the removal from library and bookshop shelves of those books which are considered to contain sexist or racist aspects.

In several countries, including the USA, Britain, China and Italy, there are children's books specifically written to present people in a non-discriminatory way. In general they appear either didactic and unashamedly propagandist or they exhibit sexism in reverse from the usual, by making the male characters ineffective. I firmly believe that creative literature cannot be written to proclaim a 'message' unless it springs from the writer's imaginative and literary talent, shaping the 'message' as an integral part of the writing. I believe also that as awareness grows and as society itself changes so there will develop as a natural progression, writers and literature that reflect the awareness and the change.

Meanwhile a consideration of sexist and racist, and any other discriminatory aspect of children's literature, should take its place beside the other criteria for evaluating and selecting children's literature.

In some countries a librarian or a teacher is made to take personal responsibility for stocking any book thought to be offensive and legal action is commonly taken to exclude the book and, in some cases, the librarian, from the library. A recent such case in the USA resulted in the Bible being found unfit for a place on the library shelves because certain sections were deemed to be concerned with pornographic sex.

Such censorship is counterbalanced by other practices which are stated in selection policy documents such as that of Hull Public Libraries. 'The only censorship is to be that established by the law of the land. No book will be excluded merely because its contents are controversial; it will be judged by other criteria'.

A stated selection policy can be a helpful foundation for library book selection if the contents are *not* rigid constraints but recommended guidelines. The benefits of such a policy statement include the following:

1. It enables everyone to know the basis of selection.
2. Responsibilities of individuals concerned with selection are assigned and clarified.
3. Criteria indicated will aid the selection process.
4. Material selected will be more effective.

A selection policy statement or guideline should cover the objectives or aims. It should define the readership in specific or general terms depending upon the circumstances. For example it may be defined as including the gifted reader, the able, the less able, the handicapped, the minority language speaker, the pre-school through teenage reader, or combinations of these for a specific school or branch library's clientele.

Knowing for whom the selection is made influences what is to be selected and this can also be included in the statement; for example fiction, information books, reference books, periodicals, pamphlets, illustrations, audio-visual materials, hardback and paperback books etc, according to the local need/finance/space available/policy requirements.

The aids to selection can be indicated, including bibliographies, reviews, critical works, selection panels, schemes for viewing actual material. Any provisos affecting selection should be stated, whether these be cost, language, theme or physical format.

The personnel concerned with selection can be indicated with a clear statement that, though several staff/teachers/students etc. may be involved in the selection process (and the more people involved the better for the usefulness of the bookstock to the readers), the decision of the librarian is final. As the professional expert, the librarian has knowledge of the needs and interests of the library clientele and knowledge of publications.

The selection policy should therefore:

1. Refer to objectives.
2. Define readership.
3. Outline selection personnel.
4. Specify materials by type and level.
5. Identify provisos in terms of quantity, quality criteria, finance, areas of controversy.
6. Outline methods of and aids to selection.

Children's literature awards
The selection of children's literature for awards is part of a very complex field where rules, criteria, rewards and effects vary considerably from country to country and from one award to another.

It is clear that in those countries where there is a large amount of children's literature there is also a range of children's book awards, as demonstrated in the select list given later in the chapter.

The basic aspects that need to be considered when either creating awards or assessing them include the following:

1. Rules of entry e.g. eligibility in terms of nationality, date of publication, type of literature, children's age group.
2. Terms of award e.g. the best literary book/outstanding book in any year, best total work, most popular book, outstanding illustration, outstanding information book,

new talent, best on a theme, most socially useful, best translation or outstanding contribution to the world of children's literature.
3. Nominations e.g. via publisher, librarian, reader.
4. Judges e.g. writers, librarians, publishers, literary critics, graphic experts, children.
5. Methods of assessment e.g. procedures, timescale, individual and collective judging.
6. Criteria for selection, related to the terms of the award.
7. Value of the award e.g. medal, money or prestige, or all of these.
8. Possible effects of awards e.g. raising the standards of writing and illustration; encouraging writers and illustrators; rewarding merit; giving recognition and publicity to the children's book world; providing a basis for quality collections of children's literature.

The list that follows contains examples of national and international awards for children's literature. Their rules, criteria and rewards vary and are too many and too complicated to be included here. Unless otherwise stated the awards are for excellence in children's literature, usually selected from the publications of any one year.

Selected examples of children's book awards

Australia	Children's Book of the Year Award; A for children's book, B for picture book.
Austria	State Prize for Young People's Literature. Vienna Children's and Youth's Book Prize.
Canada	Book of the Year for Children Medal. Canadian Children's Book Award. Canadian Library Association Best French Children's Book.
Czechoslovakia	Marie Majerova Prizes 1. Writer, 2. Illustrator, for their lifework in children's books.

Denmark	Danish Prize for Children's and Youth Books.
France	Enfance du Monde Prize. Fantasia Prize. Grand Prize for Children's Literature. Grand Prize for Youth Literature.
Germany (GDR)	East German Youth Organization Prize.
Germany (FDR)	German Juvenile Book Award.
Greece	Greek National Prize.
Israel	Ben-Yitzhak Award (for Illustration).
Japan	Sankei Award. Owl Prize for illustration (chosen by visitors' to the children's book exhibition).
Netherlands	Dutch Prize for the Best Children's Books.
Norway	Damm Prize. Children's and Youth Book Award. Norwegian State Prize.
Poland	Janus Korezak Prize. The Eagle's Feather (awarded by teenagers for their favourite writer).
Sweden	Nils Holgersson Medal.
Switzerland	Swiss Teachers' Association Youth Book Prize.
United Kingdom	Carnegie Medal. Kathleen Fidler Award (for young Scottish writers). Greenaway Award (for illustration). Guardian Award. Times Educational Supplement Information Book Award. Other Award (for literary merit plus a balanced picture of sex roles, race or occupation etc). Mother Goose Award (for most exciting newcomer to children's book illustration). Whitbread Literary Award.
USA	Newbery Medal. Caldecott Medal (for illustration). Laura Ingalls Wilder Award. National Book Award for Children's Literature. Mildred Batchelder Award (for translation). National Council of Teachers of English Award (for excellence in poetry for Children).

140

International awards

IBBY (International Board on Books for Young People) organizes the *Hans Christian Andersen Awards* every two years; one for an author and one for an illustrator whose works form an outstanding body of literature. *International Jane Addams Children's Book Award* is given by the Women's International League for Peace and Freedom and the Jane Addams Peace Foundation. *International Reading Association Award* is given annually to an author showing unusual promise in children's book writing. Two awards are given at the Bologna Book Fair, an international event. *Critici in Erba Prize* is given for the best illustrated book and is selected by a jury of children. The *Graphic Prize* goes to a children's and young people's book considered best from a technical and graphic viewpoint by a jury of experts.

Awards for Services to the World of Children's Literature

Examples include the *Eleanor Farjeon Award* in Britain, the *Spanish National Prize* in Spain and the *Constance Lindsay Skinner Award* in USA. These are awarded to researchers, critics, lecturers, promoters of children's literature in organizations and areas, and who in many cases also write books for or about children and their books.

Whatever form of evaluation or selection of children's books takes place it involves consideration of the objectives, the needs, interests and abilities of child readers, and the literary criteria, graphic quality and production. It requires also an understanding of the place of each book in comparison with others in the world of children's literature, an understanding which develops with knowledge and experience.

Further readings

Crouch, Marcus and Ellis, Alex. *Chosen for Children*. London, Library Association, 3rd. ed. 1977

Dixon, Bob. *Catching Them Young*. 2 vols. London, Pluto Press, 1977

Fader, Daniel and McNeill, Elton *Hooked on Books*. London, Pergamon, 1969

Marshall, Margaret R. *Libraries and the Handicapped Child*. London, Deutsch, 1981

Stinton, Judith ed. *Racism and Sexism in Children's Books*. London, Writers and Readers Publications Group, 1980

CHAPTER NINE

Bibliographical Aids to Children's Literature

The bibliography of children's literature in the English language is extensive and there are many sources of information in other languages. The functions of bibliography involve identifying, listing, describing, evaluating, comparing, analysing, criticizing, promoting and publicising and each of these aspects can be found in one or other kind of bibliographical aid concerned with children's literature.

Some are intended to be part of the general critical apparatus of any literature, others are guides for the student of children's books, others provide information for those who select children's books. Bibliographical works in the English language can be categorized in the following way and some examples are given in each category:

1. *Histories of children's literature and children's book illustration*
These chart with varying emphases, the development of books for children. For example F. J. Harvey Darton's *Children's Books in England; Five Centuries of Social Life* (Cambridge, C.U.P., 1958) is a scholarly detailed study relating the books to the life in each period and is considered to be the standard work. Similarly detailed but with an American emphasis is Cornelia Meigs' *A Critical History of Children's Literature; a Survey of Children's Books in English From Earliest Times to the Present* (New York, Macmillan, rev. ed. 1970). John Rowe Townsend's *Written For Children* (London, Kestrel, 1974) is a readable introduction

to the subject and Alec Ellis's *A History of Children's Reading and Literature* (London, Pergamon, 1968) provides the background to aspects of school and leisure reading in their historical settings.

'An awareness of the development of children's literature in every country where it presently exists' is the subtitle of Anne Pellowski's *The World of Children's Literature* (New York, Bowker, 2nd ed., 1968).

The development of children's book illustration is also a subject for historical coverage, though there is much less material published than for the textual aspects. This is possibly because of the very wide range of art work and probably because of the high cost of reproducing illustrations, an essential part of any book on illustration.

Basic examples include the standard works covering the period up to 1955. These are Bertha Mahoney Miller and others, *Illustrators of Children's Books, 1744–1945*; Ruth Hill Viguers and others, *Illustrators of Children's Books, 1946–1956*; and Lee Kingman and others, *Illustrators of Children's Books, 1957–1966*, all published by Hornbook Inc. of Boston in 1947, 1968 and 1979 respectively. Emphasis on European children's book illustration is found in Bettina Hurlimann's *Picture Book World* (London, O.U.P., 1967).

In addition to complete books on the theme there are hundreds of references to illustration in books about children's literature and hundreds of articles on many aspects of writers, books, children's periodicals throughout the ages in journals connected with literature, art, librarianship and education. Such articles can be identified through periodical indexes and abstracting media.

2. Critical works
There is a very large amount of literary criticism and descrip-

tion of children's books in many countries and it falls into a number of categories. For instance there are the selections of articles or papers collected into book form, as in *Children and Literature; views and reviews*, edited by Virginia Haviland (London, The Bodley Head, 1974) and *The Cool Web; the pattern of children's reading*, edited by Margaret Meek (London, The Bodley Head, 1977), which together form a very readable and wide coverage of the writer, the book, the illustrator, the reviewer, the critic, and the children's book world. Similarly papers given at conferences can provide in collected form a range of information and attitude on a theme as in *Through Folklore to Literature*, papers presented at the Australian National Section of IBBY Conference on Children's Literature in 1978, edited by Maurice Saxby (Sydney, IBBY Australia Publications, 1979).

Then there is an individual's coverage of the kinds of children's book as in Sheila Ray's *Children's Fiction* (London, Brockhampton, 1970), or one particular aspect as in Elizabeth Cook's *The Ordinary and the Fabulous* (London, C.U.P., 1976) which looks at myth, legend and fairy tales; or one particular author, as in Sheila Ray's *The Blyton Phenomenon* (London, Deutsch, 1982).

There is the critical discussion of one particular genre as in Margery Fisher's *Matters of Fact; aspects of non-fiction for children* (London, Hodder & Stoughton, 1972) or Margaret R. Marshall's *Libraries and Literature for Teenagers* (London, Deutsch, 1975). Analysis and discussion are also found in books about authors and their works, in relation to children and reading needs and interests, as in *Children and Books* by Zena Sutherland and May Hill Arbuthnot (New York, Scott, Foresman, 5th ed., 1977) and Dorothy Butler's *Babies Need Books* London, Bodley Head, 1980). An example from a non-English speaking country is Efrain Subero's *La Literature Infantil Venezeulana; estudio y bibliografia* (Venezuelan Children's Literature; study and bibliography) (Caracas, Centro de Cepacitacian Docente de El Macaro, 1977).

3. *Biographies and autobiographies of authors and illustrators and other book people*

These vary from short monographs to full length biographies and autobiographies, and from discursive treatment to quick reference dictionary treatment. For instance the Bodley Head Monograph Series includes Margaret Meek's *Rosemary Sutcliff* (London, Bodley Head, 1962). Individual biographies include Margaret Lane's *The Tale of Beatrix Potter* (London, Warne, 1968) and Paul Binding's *Robert Louis Stevenson* (London, O.U.P., 1974).

Encyclopaedic works of biography are exemplified by *Twentieth Century Children's Writers*, edited by D. L. Kirkpatrick (London, Macmillan, 1978). Autobiographical material is more often found in periodical articles and there are thousands of these on a wide range of authors and illustrators. An autobiographical work which reveals not only the biographee but also books in action is the acclaimed *Cushla and Her Books* by Dorothy Butler (London, Hodder & Stoughton, 1979) describing the development of a multiply handicapped girl and her reading interests stimulated by her grandmother, Mrs Butler and Cushla's parents.

4. *Bibliographies, lists and indexes*

In order to have co-ordinated and comprehensive information about the existence of children's literature and works about children's books it is necessary to locate, identify and then list what is found. The most comprehensive such list ought to be the national bibliography. Many countries have such a bibliography and others are in the process of compiling a bibliography of children's literature as part of the national bibliography. Britain lags behind in that as though there is a national bibliography there is not a separate section from which all items identified as relevant to children's literature could be extracted quickly for use. *British National Bibliography* (BNB) cumulates from weekly issues to annual volumes but children's literature is identified only at Dewey 823.91 J. Non-fiction, poetry, drama and works about children's literature are all listed separately from the children's fiction and cannot be identified as for children, without prior knowledge.

Other lists exist on a commercial basis such as *Children's Books in Print* (New York, Bowker 198–), Marcie Muir's *Bibliography of Australian Children's Books* (London, Deutsch, 1970 and 1976). Similar listing for special aspects can be found in *Junior Fiction Index* edited by Patricia M. Frend (London, Association of Assistant Librarians, 3rd ed., 1977) in which titles are arranged under subject headings; *Sequels, vol. 2, Junior Books*, compiled by Frank M. Gardner and Lisa Christina Persson (A.A.L. 1976) lists about 7,000 titles which involve a sequel.

A special aspect list which is also a checklist to the holdings of the Commonwealth Institute's Library and Resource Centre in London, is the 56 page *Commonwealth Children's Literature* (Checklists on Commonwealth Literature No. 1. London Commonwealth Institute, 1979).

5. *Catalogues*
Allied to the listing in the previous section which tends to be overall in content, are the published catalogues of:

a. libraries, such as the British Museum Catalogue, in which again, children's books are not listed separately, and the Library of Congress Catalogue, in which there *is* ease of access to children's books; the Swedish Institute for Children's Books publishes a catalogue of the reference collection.

b. special collections such as that of the Osborne Collection in Boys and Girls House, Toronto, Canada, and the collection of Children's Books in the Rare Books Division of the Library of Congress.

c. exhibitions, such as Brian Alderson's *Catalogue of the Exhibition of Pictures by Maurice Sendak* (London, Bodley Head, 1976).

d. publishers, where the intention behind the catalogue is to publicize the backlist and the new publications, for intending purchasers.

e. booksellers, particularly secondhand and rare book shops which often sell early children's books by mail via the catalogue or duplicated list.

f. stock catalogues of library suppliers who do business with library systems at home and abroad.

g. miscellaneous catalogues such as the dissertation order service supplied by University Microfilms International (Ann Arbor and London) entitled *Doctoral Dissertations on Children's Literature* and described under the heading of 10. Theses.

6. *Guides to the literature*

Similar listings are found in the, usually, select lists to aspects of children's literature of books for age groups or interests or needs. These may be produced by individual libraries for local use or by organization or individual for wider use. British examples include the Youth Libraries Group publications, such as *Ghostly Encounters* (London, Library Association Y.L.G. Pamphlet no. 19, n.d.); National Book League publications such as *Fantasy Books For Children* selected by Naomi Lewis (London, N.B.L., 1977); School Library Association publications such as *Seeing Clear; Books for the Partially Sighted Child* compiled by Margaret R. Marshall (Oxford, S.L.A., 1977); or the American Library Association publications such as *Notes for a Different Drummer; a guide to juvenile fiction portraying the handicapped*, compiled by Barbara Baskin (A.L.A.,

1977). Individual guides include examples such as Jeanette Hotchkiss' *African-Asian Reading Guide* (Metuchen, Scarecrow, 1976) and *Das Buch der Jugend* which is an annual list containing a selection of books recommended as the basic stock for a school library or children's department of a public library, by the Arbeitkreis für Jugendliteratur in Germany; *Libros Infantiles Y Juveniles en España 1960–1975* (Children's and Youth Books in Spain, 1960–1975) (Madrid, Instituto Nacional del Libro Espanol, 1976).

Most national libraries, children's literature research centres, librarianship organizations, public library children's departments and school libraries compile guides for parents, researchers, librarians, educationalists or for the children themselves, and the content, style of entry and annotative or evaluative or descriptive information in the guide will be determined by which of these groups is the intended readership.

Some countries produce annual lists of the best of the year's publications, as in *Children's Books of the Year*, selected for many years by Elaine Moss for the National Book League in UK and currently by Barbara Sherrard Smith; and *Notable Children's Books for 19—*selected by the Children's Services Division of the American Library Association.

Then there is the catalogue of the best from 57 countries or languages, *The Best of the Best* edited by Walter Scherf, Director of the International Youth Library in Munich. The most recent edition was in 1976 published by Verlag Dokumentation.

7. Periodicals
Compared with the quantity of journals relevant to adult literature and reading there are few periodical publications concerned with children's literature. Most countries have at

least one vehicle for publishing views or reviews of children's books and those who work with children and books are usually avid readers of such journals. Periodical publications can be divided into the following sections:

a. Literary journals such as *Signal; approaches to children's books*, edited by Nancy Chambers, quarterly, Thimble Press; *Children's Literature in Education*, an international quarterly with an Anglo-American editorial board.

b. Journals with critical articles and review sections such as *Hornbook Magazine*, edited bi-monthly by Ethel Heins, *Top of the News*, produced monthly by the Children's Services Division of the American Library Association, and the international journal *Bookbird*, issued by the International Board on Books for Young People and the International Institute for Children's Literature and Reading Research in Vienna, Austria.

c. Journals covering children's literature and librarianship or education, such as the American *School Library Journal*, issued monthly; the British *School Librarian*, issued quarterly by the School Library Association and the Australian *Review*, issued quarterly by the School Libraries Branch of the Education Department of South Australia; *Books For Keeps*, issued six times a year by the School Bookshop Association in London; *The Use of English*, a quarterly journal and *Reading*, the quarterly journal of the International Reading Association.

d. Review journals specifically concerned with reviewing children's books: English language examples include *Growing Point*, edited by Margery Fisher in 9 issues a year; *Junior Bookshelf* in 6 issues a year; *Books For Your Children*, a magazine for parents, quarterly. *The Bulletin of the Center for Children's Books* is edited by

Zena Sutherland in Chicago monthly, and *Booklist* is edited by Betsy Hearne for the American Library Association twice a month.

e. Book journals and supplements: these are exemplified by the Children's Book Supplement quarterly in the monthly journal *British Book News*, the publication of the British Council, and by the quarterly supplements or special issues in the *Times Literary Supplement* and the *Times Educational Supplement*. National newspapers in many countries have regular or occasional sections of children's book reviews, as do women's magazines and general periodicals.

f. Individual libraries, schools and organizations also produce their own journals or review media, usually for local use.

g. Journals in non-English language countries, e.g. the Dutch *En Nu Over Jeugdliteratuur*, The Hague, N.B.L.C. six times a year.

8. Abstracts

These can take several forms and cover general or specific aspects of the children's book world. Perhaps the most specific internationally is *Children's Literature Abstracts* edited by Colin Ray in UK for IFLA as a quarterly service.

Two American works abstract reviews of children's books: *Book Review Digest*, published by Wilson ten times a year and containing reviews of books published in USA and reviewed in the past one and a half years, and *Children's Literature Review*, published by Gale of Detroit twice a year and containing excerpts from reviews and critical commentary.

Of the several general abstracting works which include in their coverage aspects of children's literature and reading, three examples are *Library and Information Science Abstracts* (LISA) provided by the Library Association in Britain; *Library Literature*, provided in USA by H. W. Wilson, both of which cover a wide variety of the world's professional librarianship periodical literature; and the more general abstract *British Humanities Index*, published by the Library Association in UK, in which articles on children's literature are abstracted from a wide range of general, educational and literary journals.

9. Reference works

From the mass of publications that can be used to dip into for specific information only a sample can be included here: *Who's Who in Children's Books; a treasury of the familiar characters of childhood*, compiled by Margery Fisher (London, Weidenfeld & Nicolson, 1975); *Where's That Poem?* compiled by Helen Morris (London, Blackwell, 1979) lists poems by title and subject with sources in books of poetry. *The Dobler World Directory of Youth Periodicals* (New York, Citation Press, 3rd ed., 1970) lists subject periodicals of interest to young people; *Twentieth Century Children's Writers*, edited by D. L. Kirkpatrick (London, Macmillan, 1978) has informative biographical and critical entries for hundreds of writers.

10. Theses etc.

The considerable amount of research being undertaken by students of children's literature at all levels in many countries is not as well documented and available as it could be, so that any evidence of its existence is welcome. In addition to general works such as the annual publication *Index to Theses* (London, Aslib) there are specialist sources such as *Radials Bulletin*, Research and Development, Information and Library Science, published twice a year (London, Library Association); Peter L. Hunt's *Children's Book Research in Britain; research in British institutions of higher education on children's books and related subjects* (Cardiff, UWIST,

Dept. of English, 1977); *Phaedrus*; an international journal of children's literature research edited by James Fraser (P.O. Box 1166, Marblehead, Mass., 01945, USA); *Doctoral Dissertations in Children's Literature*, a catalogue of a selection of dissertations recently submitted to North American universities (Ann Abor, University Microfilms International); and D. L. Monson and B. J. Peltola's *Research in Children's Literature, annotated bibliography* (Newark, Del., International Reading Association, 1976).

11. *Miscellaneous*
There are many such items throughout the world – papers presented at conferences, reports, surveys, lists, publicity leaflets, guides to libraries and institutions concerned with children and a wide range of books connected with the use of children's and youth books in school and society; such as Frank Whitehead's survey of thousands of children and their reading interests and habits, published as *Children and Their Books* (Schools Council Research Project, London, Macmillan, 1977); John L. Foster's *Reluctant to Read* (London, Ward Lock Educational, 1977) and Robert Carlsen's *Books and the Teenage Reader* (New York, Harper & Row, 2nd rev. ed., 1980).

Guides to using books in class projects and in library use instruction; aids to book selection for the gifted and the handicapped; information for parents and teachers and librarians – all these are too numerous to be listed in this book. Much is only of local use, some is ephemeral, but their presence can be indicated here as a part of the mass of material that can be labelled 'bibliographical sources'.

CHAPTER TEN

Promoting Children's Books in Libraries

The need to promote children's books raises at least two questions – *why* promote children's literature and *how* can children's literature be promoted?

The first question can be answered by a number of suggested benefits;

1. *Benefit to the child reader*
   a. The child is exposed through reading, to the possibility of development of the following; the thought processes, the imagination, the intellect, vocabulary, language, social and emotional stimulation, knowledge, mental and visual perception.
   b. Through books the child has access to society's thoughts and experiences, and through the skills of reading the child can take part in the practical aspects required of a member of a literate society, for example reading notices, instructions, official forms. Both aspects set firm foundations for the future adult.
   c. Children are unlikely to see the full range of children's books unless it is brought to their attention by one means or another, and unlikely to find particular books needed unless help is available.

2. *Benefit to the adult users of children's books*
Promotion is needed in order to inform adults who need children's books for their own purposes or for use with children. The majority of adults are parents selecting with or on

154

behalf of their children, and teachers selecting for library purposes or for class use. Children's book people needing books for study and research purposes are frequent users of various kinds of library or collection. But within a community there are many adults and organizations concerned with children, and the promotion of children's books to them can be of benefit to the children they serve.

The following is a composite list from information given by thirty children's librarians from many parts of UK who attended a course on children's libraries and the community. They were asked to name the organizations with which they liaised professionally in their community:

schools
playgroups and nursery schools
guides, scouts, brownies
women's organizations
probation offices (for delinquent youth)
toy libraries
mentally handicapped societies and similar
community relations groups
family reading schemes
adult literacy schemes
mother and baby clubs and clinics
hospital and home tutors
hospitals
prisons and detention centres
field study centres
Tufty clubs (road safety for children)
nursery nurses courses
child assessment centres
colleges of education
colleges of librarianship
social services departments
residential care associations

155

youth clubs
adventure playground supervisors
youth workers
pressure groups
careers officers
summer play schemes
local children's book groups
teachers centres
local history societies
museum services
ethnic language schools
and the various education bodies such as curriculum
 development centres, school library association, teaching trade unions and parent/teacher associations.

3. Benefits to the library

Where the library is a public library, a school library or a specialist collection, it is wasteful if the books are on the shelves unused or little used. Highlighting kinds of book by one means or another will bring them to the attention of those in the library. Promotion outside the library will inform the wider community. This is likely to make the books cost-effective and will therefore indicate to those who provide the book funds that the money is well spent and that more money, or at least a continuation of funds, is worthwhile.

Promotion of children's books in libraries is important because the very existence of the library is vital. It provides:

a. a link with the whole of human knowledge and experience
b. an opportunity for self education or to complement school education
c. availability of choice
d. a place and a time to read voluntarily

156

e. a loan facility
f. a community focal point
g. enjoyment and therefore motivation to read more.

4. Benefits to the nation's literary health

Librarians must meet with teachers, writers, publishers, booksellers and educationalists to give the widest possible publicity to the need for books and related materials for children and the need for bibliographic help for those attempting to provide a book service for children.

Between them they can point to the need for national co-ordination and promotion of children's book services and to the importance of co-operation at all levels within a country.

Such meetings can be arranged in the form of conferences, one-day schools, workshops, committees, or informal invitations to discussion. They should not only be the opportunity to share views and information and experiences but also an occasion for creating or re-inforcing a policy, planning a course of action, encouraging translation and the creation of indigenous children's books.

They can be sponsored by local members of international groups such as the International Federation of Library Associations (IFLA) or the International Board on Books For Young People (IBBY), or the Regional Book Development Centres of Unesco, such as the Regional Book Development Centre for Africa South of the Sahara, in Yaoundé, Cameroon, or the Centre for Latin America in Bogota, Colombia.

Meetings can be arranged by national groups such as the Library Association or the School Library Association or national book organizations; or by educational institutions such as schools of librarianship or schools of education for teachers. Training officers in individual library systems or education authorities can include courses on children's

157

books in their in-service programmes. Enthusiastic individuals in the world of children's books may call together other interested people.

The second aspect of *how* to promote children's books is partly answered by this last point. Means of promotion are dependent upon the promoter's knowledge of children's books and needs. Keeping children's book people informed and enabling them to co-operate increases the chances of effective promotion. So in addition to this the following suggestions are offered:

1. *General activities, national and local*
   a. meetings of all interested in children and books
   b. exhibitions of children's books, illustrations and related materials, general, thematic, or for the needs of special ages, conditions or groups of children
   c. creation of children's libraries in public libraries, schools, playgroups, community centres, or book box services or travelling libraries
   d. establishment of regional and national libraries of children's books, and national centres of study and research into children's books
   e. liaison with organizations and individuals for the specific furtherance of knowledge and services
   f. translation of children's books into national or local vernacular.
   g. use of radio, television and press for publicity and information about children's books
   h. organization of national book weeks

2. *Specific activities in the local library and community library and school library*
These would be undertaken by librarians, teachers, volunteers or others, depending upon the local circumstances.

   a. display of books, periodicals, pictures, toys, games and

other materials extracted from the stock in order to publicize its existence or to back up a topical event or a study theme

b. library guiding by shelf labels, tier guides, location guides, wall charts, posters, use of the catalogue, notices etc. to facilitate ease of access to the books

c. booklists of new acquisitions, for age or interest groups and for school projects, to enable children (or adults) to know what is available in the library on those aspects

d. library instruction on what is in the library, how to find it, how to use it and how to get the most out of books now and in the future

e. children's library magazine, to provide a vehicle for children's own creative writing and to give book and library news

f. storytelling, to introduce to children books, excerpts, poems and pictures that they might not otherwise read or see; to whet the appetite for reading; to provide a stimulus for developing the skill of listening; adding to vocabulary, imaginative experience and knowledge; aiding identification; offering a valuable *group* experience of books

g. library reading clubs; some provide lists of books to be read, towards a badge or star or other reward; some are family schemes where parents and children and librarian read a specified book together and discuss it; some are aimed at particular kinds of book as with the Science Fiction Club or the Poetry Club organized by some libraries

h. activities in the library, such as art hobby groups, talks by specialists, brains trusts and quizzes, film shows, handicraft hours, concerts and music sessions, puppet groups, competitions, are all designed to interest the reader on a wider scale

    i. visits to the local library by classes of school children from local schools, both to introduce them to the library service and to choose books

    j. parent/child clubs, in which pre-school children and their parents, or ethnic groups read and talk and play

    k. paperback and swap shops, whereby children bring their own finished or unwanted books and exchange (or swap) them for something different, from the shelf set aside for this purpose

    l. a school bookshop or other bookselling agency as described in Chapter Four

    m. parents' bookshelf in school or public library

    n. time in school to read for pleasure

    o. reading week in which authors, publishers, printers, booksellers etc. describe their work; reading encouraged

    p. holiday programmes in the library and outside

    q. advice to individual children and adults

3. *Specific promotion activities in the community*

    a. through liaison with all organizations and groups concerned with children, by publicity, public relations and provision of books and advice

    b. talking about books to children in school, in youth clubs and other organizations where children and young people are

    c. talking about books to adults in their organizations and their conferences and courses

    d. storytelling in public places, possibly using bus, boat or train for book activities where appropriate, and mobile libraries with generators for film shows

    e. organizing displays of books at local festivals, fairs and shows

    f. using the local press, radio and television and any other communication media locally to promote books and libraries.

All the suggestions listed are activities that are carried out in many countries in many libraries, but a decision on which to employ for most effective promotion of books rests on a number of factors, such as the nature of the local community, gecgraphical distribution of the population, transport facilities, availability of electricity and equipment, the age range of children in the locality, school and organization links. These factors would be taken into consideration in the forward planning along with time, space, bookstock, personnel and cost factors.

The basic aspects without which promotion cannot take place, are an adequate range and number of books, and enthusiastic and knowledgeable book people.

These factors express the whole concept of the children's book world; encouragement to writers and artists to create children's books, encouragement to make them available, and encouragement to children to read and enjoy.

Further readings
Bauer, Caroline F. Handbook For Storytellers, Chicago, A.L.A. 1977

Bernstein, Joanne ed. *Books to Help Children Cope with Separation and Loss* New York, Bowker, 1977

Butler, Dorothy. *Babies Need Books*. London, Bodley Head, 1980

Colwell, Eileen. *Storytelling*. London, Bodley Head, 1980

Fader, Daniel and McNeill, Elton B. *Hooked on Books*. London, Pergamon, 1969

Fletcher, G. R. and Jenkins F. Books at Work in Cleveland. *Assistant Librarian* 70(12) Dec. 1977 pp. 191–194

Kennerley, Peter. *Running a School Bookshop; theory and practice*. London, Ward Lock, Ed., 1978

Patte, Geneviève. *Laissez-les Lire; les enfants et les bibliothèques*. Paris, Ed. Ouvrières, 1978

Pellowski, Anne. *Made to Measure; children's books in developing countries*. Paris, Unesco, 1980
The World of Storytelling. London and New York, Bowker, 1977

Polette, Nancy and Hamlin, Marjorie. *Exploring Books with Gifted Children*. New York, Libraries Unlimited, 1980

Roberts, Lorna. *The 1980 Bookmaster Scheme*. London, Westminster City Libraries, 1981

Wertheimer, Leonard ed. Library Services to ethno-cultural minorities. *Library Trends*, Fall 29 (2) 1980 whole issue.

Local and national periodicals concerned with children's literature and children's libraries.

Bibliographical Information

Most of the books listed on the following pages are in the English language and most of the titles and publishers given are those for the United Kingdom. But many of the books appear also in other countries though both title and publisher may change when a book is translated and/or published in a country other than that of its original publication.

At the end of each chapter further readings are shown. These were selected to provide a stepping-stone to more detailed discussion of the theme of the chapter.

There now follows;

A. List of children's books referred to in the text
B. Books about children's books
C. Select list of children's literature periodicals

A. Children's Books Referred to in the Text
Adams, Richard. *Watership Down*. London, Kestrel, 1976
Aesop. *Aesop's Fables*. ed. by G. Beal. London, Angus & Robertson, 1977
Ahlberg, Janet and Allan. *Old Joke Book*. London, Kestrel, 1976
   Burglar Bill. London, Heinemann, 1977
Alcott, Louisa May. *Little Women*. London, Blackie, 1971
Alexander, Lloyd. *Black Cauldron, Book of Three, Castle of Lyr, High King, Taran Wanderers*. London, Collins, 1973–1979
Allen, Daniel M. *The New American Poetry*. New York, Grove, 1960
Althea. *What is a Union?* Cambridge, Dinosaur, 1981

Andersen, Hans Christian. *Classic fairy tales*. Trans. by Erik Haugaard. London, Gollancz, 1976

Anno, Mitsumasa. *Anno's Alphabet*. London, Bodley Head, 1972

The King's Flower. London, Bodley Head, 1979

Arabian Nights' Entertainments, ed. by Annabel Williams-Ellis. London, Blackie, 1977

Arundel, Honor. *Two Sisters*. London, Heinemann, 1968

The Blanket Word. London, Hamilton, 1973

Ashley, Bernard. *Terry on the Fence*. London, O.U.P., 1975

The Trouble with Donovan Croft. London, O.U.P., 1974

Asimov, Isaac. *The Best of Isaac Asimov*. London, Sphere, 1977

Bagnold, Enid. *National Velvet*. London, Heinemann, 1935

Baines, Talbot. *Fifth Form at St Dominic's*. out of print

Barrie, J. M. *Peter Pan*. London, Hodder & Stoughton, 1979

Beckman, Gunnel. *Mia*. trans. by Joan Tate. London, Bodley Head, 1974

Beckman, Thea. *Stad in de Storm* (Town in a storm). Rotterdam, Lenniscaat, 1979

Beresford, Elizabeth. *The Wombles*. London, Benn, 1968

Berrisford, Judith M. *Jackie and the Pony Boys*. London, Collins, 1973

Blakeley, Peggy. *The Great Big Book of Nursery Rhymes*. London, Black, 1978

Blishen, Edward ed. *Oxford Book of Poetry for Children*, London, O.U.P., 1963.

Blume, Judy. *Forever*. London, Gollancz, 1976

Blyton, Enid. *Castle of Adventure*. London, Macmillan, 1946

Five on a Treasure Island, London, Hodder & Stoughton, 1979

The Island of Adventure. London, Macmillan, 1944

The Naughtiest Girl in the School. London, Hamlyn, 1979

Second Form at St Clare's and *Second Form at Malory Towers*. London, Hamlyn, 1979

Bond, Michael. *Paddington Bear*. London, Collins, 1972

Boston, Lucy M. *The Sea-Egg*. London, Faber, 1970

Boylston, Helen. *Sue Barton, Rural Nurse*. London, Brock-hampton, 1971

Bradbury, Ray. *Fahrenheit 451*. London, Hart-Davis, 1954

Branfield, John. *Nancecuke*. London, Hutchinson Ed., 1974

Brazil, Angela. *School on the Loch*. London, Collins, 1969

Brent-Dyer, Elinor. *Exploits of the Chalet Girls*. London, Collins, 1972

Briggs, Raymond. *Father Christmas*. London, Hamilton, 1973

Fungus the Bogeyman. London, Hamilton, 1977

The Mother Goose Treasury. London, Hamilton, 1966

Browne, Anthony. *A Walk in the Park*. London, Hamilton, 1977

Through the Magic Mirror. London, Hamilton, 1976

Bruna, Dick. *My Vest is White*. London, Methuen, 1976

Brychta, Alex. *Numbers One to Ten and Back Again*. N.Y. Frank Bk. 1977

Buckeridge, Anthony. *According to Jennings*. London, Collins, 1972

Bunyan, John. *Pilgrim's Progress*. London, Dent, 1954

Burke, Susan. *Alexander in Trouble*. London, Bodley Head, 1979

Burnford, Sheila. *The Incredible Journey*. London, Hodder & Stoughton, 1975

Burningham, John. *Mr Gumpy's Outing*. London, Cape, 1970

Byars, Betsy. *The Eighteenth Emergency*. London, Bodley Head, 1974

Carroll, Lewis. *Alice in Wonderland*. London, Bodley Head, 1974

Causeley, Charles. *Collected Poems*. London, Macmillan, 1975

Chambers, Aidan. *Breaktime*. London, Bodley Head, 1978

Christie, Agatha. *Miss Marple's Final Cases and others*. London, Collins, 1979

Children as Writers. London, W. H. Smith, annual.

Christopher, John. *Lotus Caves*. London, Hamilton, 1969

Cleary, Beverley. *Fifteen*. London, Penguin, 1977

165

Cole, William comp. *Oh What Nonsense*. London, Methuen, 1968

Cooper, Susan. *Dark is Rising*. London, Chatto, 1973

Cormier, Robert. *The Chocolate War*. London, Gollancz, 1975

Cresswell, Helen. *The Nightwatchmen*. London, Penguin, 1976

Crompton, Richmal. *William in Trouble*. London, Collins, 1971

Crossley-Holland, Kevin. *Book of Northern Legends*. London, Faber, 1977

Cumming, Primrose. *Silver Snaffles*. London, Hodder & Stoughton, 1976

Defoe, Daniel. *Robinson Crusoe*. London, Dent, 1954

De Jong, Meindert. *House of Sixty Fathers*. London, Penguin, 1971

Dickinson, Peter. *Devil's Children*. London, Gollancz, 1970
Weathermonger. London, Gollancz, 1968

Edwards, Dorothy. *My Naughty Little Sister*. London, Methuen, 1969

Edwards, Monica. *Rennie Goes Riding*. London, Hodder & Stoughton, 1979

Eliot, T. S. *Old Possum's Book of Practical Cats*. London, Faber, 1975

Enright, Elizabeth. *The Saturdays*. London, Heinemann, 1964

Estes, Eleanor. *Ginger Pye*. London, Bodley Head, 1972

Ferguson, Ruby. *Jill's Riding Club*. London, Brockhampton, 1969

Fisk, Nicholas. *Time Trap*. London, Gollancz, 1976

Fitzhugh, Louise. *Nobody's Family is Going to Change*. London, Gollancz, 1976

Fleming, Ian. *Diamonds Are Forever*. London, Cape, 1956

Foreman, Michael. *All the King's Horses*. London, Hamilton, 1976

Fox, Paula. *How Many Miles to Babylon?* London, Macmillan, 1968

French, Fiona. *Aio the Rainmaker*. London, O.U.P., 1975

Fuchs, Ursula. *Emma Oder Die Unruhige Zeit* (Emma or the Restless Times). Modantel-Neunkirchen, Anrich, 1979

Gag, Wanda. *Millions of Cats*. London, Faber, 1929

Gallico, Paul. *Snow Goose*. London, Joseph, 1969

Garfield, Leon and Blishen, Ward. *God Beneath the Sea*. London, Longman, 1970

Garfield, Leon. *Devil-in-the-Fog*. London, Longman, 1966

Garner, Alan. *Owl Service*. London, Collins, 1967

Goscinny and Uderzo. *Asterix in Spain*. trans by Anthea Bell and D. Hockridge. London, Hodder & Stoughton, 1971

Grahame, Kenneth. *The Wind in the Willows*. London, Methuen, 1971

Gray, J. E. B. *Indian Tales and Legends*. London, O.U.P., 1979

Grimm, J. C. and W. K. *Fairy Tales*. ed. by Annabel Williams-Ellis. London, Blackie, 1977

Gripe, Maria. *Hugo*. trans. by Paul Britten Austin. London, Chatto, 1971

Hallworth, Grace. *Listen to This Story; tales from the West Indies*. London, Methuen, 1978

Harris, Mary. *The Bus Girls*. London, Faber, 1965

Hartley, L. P. *The Go-Between*. London, Hamilton, 1953

Haviland, Virginia, ed. *The Faber Book of North American Legends*. London, Faber, 1979

Hay, Dean. *Things in the Kitchen*. London, Collins, 1976

Heide, Florence Parry. *The Shrinking of Treehorn*. London, Kestrel, 1975

Heinlein, Robert. *Tunnel in the Sky*. London, Gollancz, 1965

Hendra, Judith ed. *The Illustrated Treasury of Humour for Children*. London, Hodder & Stoughton, 1981

Herge. *Tintin and the Picaros*. trans. by Leslie Lonsdale Cooper and Michael Turner. London, Methuen, 1976

Hildick, E. W. *Jim Starling*. London, Chatto, 1958

Hill, Eric. *Where's Spot*? London, Heinemann, 1980

Hines, Barry. *Kestrel for a Knave*. London, Joseph, 1974

Hinton, S. E. *Rumble Fish*. London, Gollancz, 1976

That Was Then This is Now. London, Gollancz, 1971

Hoban, Russell. *The Dancing Tiger*. London, Cape, 1979
Mouse and His Child, London, Faber, 1969
Hoke, Helen ed. *Jokes and Fun*. London, Watts, 1972
Holm, Anne. *I am David*. London, Macmillan Ed., 1978
Hughes, Langston. *Don't You Turn Back*. ed. by Lee B. Hopkins. New York, Knopf, 1969
Hughes, Monica. *Earthdark*. London, Hamilton, 1977
Hughes, Ted. *The Iron Man; A Story in Five Nights*. London, Faber, 1968
Moon-bells and Other Poems. London, Chatto, 1978
Hughes, Thomas. *Tom Brown's Schooldays*. London, Collins, 1976
Hunter, Mollie. *The Stronghold*. London, Hamilton, 1974
Ichikawa, Satomi. *The Friends*, Heinemann, 1977
From Morn to Midnight; children's verses chosen by Elaine Moss. London, Heinemann, 1977
Jacobs, Joseph. *English Fairy Tales*. London, Bodley Head, 1968
Jansson, Tove. *Finn Family Moomintroll*. London, Penguin, 1970
Jensen, Virginia Allen and Haller, Dorcas Woodbury. *What's That?* London, Collins, 1978
Jessell, Camilla. *Mark's Wheelchair Adventures*. London, Methuen, 1975
Johns, W. E. *Biggles Sorts It Out*. London, Brockhampton, 1968
Juster, Norton. *The Phantom Tollbooth*. London, Collins, 1974
Kastner, Erich. *Lottie and Lisa*. London, Cape 1950
Keats, Ezra Jack. *Peter's Chair*. (Gujerati/English edition)
The Snowy Day (Gujerati/English edition) both London, Bodley Head, 1980
Keeping, Charles. *Charley, Charlotte and the Gold Canary*. London, O.U.P., 1967
Joseph's Yard, O.U.P., 1970
Railway Passage. O.U.P., 1974
Keith, Harold. *Rifles for Watie*. Scranton, Pa., Crowell, 1957

Kingsley, Charles. *The Water Babies*. London, Allen & Unwin, 1978

Kipling, Rudyard. *The Jungle Book*. London, Macmillan, 1965

Just So Stories. London, Macmillan, 1965

Lang, Andrew. *Blue Fairy Book*. London, Kestrel, 1975

Lear, Edward. *Book of Bosh*. ed. by Brian Alderson, London, Kestrel, 1975

Le Guin, Ursula. *A Wizard of Earthsea*. London, Gollancz, 1971

L'Engle, Madeleine. *Wrinkle in Time*. London, Longman, 1963

Lewis, C. S. *The Lion the Witch and the Wardrobe*. London, Collins, 1974

Lindgren, Astrid. *Pippi Longstocking*. London, O.U.P., 1954

Lingard, Joan. *Across the Barricades*. London, Hamilton, 1972

The Clearance. London, Hamilton, 1974

Lobel, Arnold. *Frog and Toad Are Friends*. London, Worlds Work, 1971

Lofting, Hugh. *The Story of Doctor Dolittle*. London, Cape, 1968

Methuen. *Look and See Books; Bathtime*. London, Methuen, 1980

McAlpine, H. and W. *Japanese Tales and Legends*. London, O.U.P., 1958

McCord, David. *Far and Few*. New York, Dell, 1971

Macdonald, George. *Princess and Curdie*. London, Penguin, 1970

MacLean, Alistair. *When Eight Bells Toll*. London, Collins, 1966

Marryat, Frederick. *Children of the New Forest*. London, Collins, 1974

Marshall, James Vance. *Walkabout*. London, Penguin, 1969

Martin, Nancy. *Four Girls in a Store*. London, Macmillan, 1971

Mayne, William. *Blue Boat*. London, O.U.P., 1965

A Swarm in May. London, O.U.P., 1962
Milligan, Spike. *Silly Verse for Kids*. London, Dobson, 1963
Milne, A. A. *The Christopher Robin Verse Book*. London, Methuen, 1969
Winnie the Pooh. London, Methuen, 1973
Mitchnik, Helen. *Egyptian and Sudanese Folk Tales*. London, O.U.P., 1978
Montgomery, L. M. *Anne of Green Gables*. London, Harrap, 1961
Nesbit, E. M. *Five Children and It*. London, Benn, 1978
The Phoenix and the Carpet. London, Benn, 1978
The Railway Children. London, Benn, 1978
Nöstlinger, Christine. *Fly Away Home*. London, Abelard-Schuman, 1976
Norton, Andre. *Iron Cage*. London, Kestrel, 1975
Norton, Mary. *The Borrowers*. London, Dent, 1975
Nourse, Alan E. *Psi High and Others*. London, Faber, 1967
Oakley, Graham. *The Church Mice and the Moon*. London, Macmillan, 1974
O'Brien, Robert C. *Mrs Frisby and the Rats of Nimh*. London, Gollancz, 1972
Oman, Carola. *Robin Hood*. London, Dent, 1975
Opie, Iona and Peter. *The Oxford Nursery Rhyme Book*. London, O.U.P., 1955
Orwell, George. *Animal Farm*. London, Penguin, 1969
Oxenbury, Helen. *Heads, Bodies and Legs*. London, Methuen, 1980
Pearce, Philippa. *Dog So Small*. London, Longman, 1962
Tom's Midnight Garden. London, O.U.P., 1958
Perrault, Charles. *Complete Fairy Tales*. London, Longman, 1962
Peter, Diana. *Claire and Emma*. London, Black, 1976
Peyton, K. M. *Pennington's Seventeenth Summer*. London, O.U.P., 1979
The Team. London, O.U.P., 1975
Picard, Barbara Leonie. *Hero Tales from the British Isles*. London, Penguin, 1971

Pienkowski, Jan. *Haunted House*. London, Heinemann, 1979

Piers, Helen. *Rabbit is Hungry*. London, Methuen, 1978

Potter, Beatrix. *Mrs Tiggywinkle*. London, Warne, 1950

Price, Willard. *Underwater Adventure*. London, Brockhampton, 1971

Prøysen, Alf. *Mrs Pepperpot's Busy Day*. London, Hutchinson, 1970

Pullein-Thompson, Christine and Diana. *Pony to Love*. London, Pan, 1975

Ransome, Arthur. *Swallows and Amazons*. London, Penguin, 1970

Rawlings, M. *The Yearling*. London, Heinemann, 1966

Rayner, Mary. *Mr and Mrs Pig's Evening Out*. London, Macmillan, 1976

Recheis, Kathe. *Der Weite Weg des Nataiyu* (Nataiyu's Long Journey). Wien, Herder, 1978

Rees, David. *Quintin's Man*. London, Dobson, 1976

Rees, Lucy. *The Horse of Air*. London, Gaber, 1980

Richards, Frank. *Billy Bunter's Banknote*. London, Magnet Facsimiles, 1977

Riordan, James. *Tales from Central Russia*. London, Kestrel, 1976

Rodgers, Mary. *Freaky Friday*. London, Hamilton, 1973

Rodowsky, Colby. *What About Me?* London, Watt, 1977

Roffey, Maureen. *Tinker Tailor Soldier Sailor*. London, Bodley Head, 1980

Rogers, Pamela. *The Stone Angel*. London, Hamilton, 1975

Ruskin, John. *King of the Golden River*. London, Hamilton, 1978

Salkey, Andrew. *Hurricane*. London, O.U.P., 1979

Scarry, Richard. *What Do People Do All Day?* London, Collins, 1977

Sendak, Maurice. *Where the Wild Things Are*. London, Bodley Head, 1967

Serraillier, Ian. *The Silver Sword*. London, Cape, 1956

Seuss, Dr. *The Cat in the Hat*. London, Collins, 1963

Sewell, Anna. *Black Beauty*. London, Collins, 1970

Smith, Vian. *Parade of Horses*. London, Longman, 1970

Southall, Ivan. *Let the Balloon Go*. London, Methuen, 1968
To the Wild Sky. London, Angus & Robertson, 1967

Speare, Elizabeth G. *The Bronze Bow*. London, Gollancz, 1962

Spence, Eleanor. *The October Child*. London, O.U.P., 1976

Sperry, Armstrong. *The Boy Who Was Afraid*. London, Bodley Head, 1963

Spier, Peter. *The Great Flood*. London, Worlds Work, 1978

Steinbeck, John. *Red Pony*. London, Pan, 1975

Stevenson, R. L. *A Child's Garden of Verses*. London, Blackie, 1979
Treasure Island. London, Collins, 1976

Stobbs, William. *A Wide Mouthed Gaping Waddling Frog*. London, Pelham, 1977

Stratmeyer Syndicate. *The Hardy Boys, Nancy Drew* etc., London, Armada, 1979

Summerfield, Geoffrey, ed. *Voices; an anthology of poetry and pictures*. London, Penguin, 1970

Sutcliff, Rosemary. *The Light Beyond the Forest*. London, Bodley Head, 1979
Eagle of the Ninth. London, O.U.P., 1980

Swift, Jonathan. *Gulliver's Travels*. London, Collins, 1974

Thiele, Colin. *Chadwick's Chimney*. London, Methuen, 1980

Tolkien, J. R. R. *The Hobbit*. London, Allen & Unwin, 1978
The Lord of the Rings. London, Allen & Unwin, 1979

Townsend, John Rowe. *Gumble's Yard*. London, Penguin, 1970

Treadgold, Mary. *No Ponies*. London, Cape, 1979

Twain, Mark. *The Adventures of Huckleberry Finn*. London, Collins, 1978

Uden, Grant. *Dictionary of Chivalry*. London, Longman, 1968. Illus. by Pauline Baynes.

Udry, Janice M. *The Moon Jumpers*. London, Bodley Head, 1979

Untermeyer, Louis. *The Golden Treasury of Poetry*. New York, Western, 1959

Vallverdu, Joseph. *En Mir L'Esquirel* (Mir the Squirrel), Barcelona, La Galera, 1978

Verne, Jules. *20,000 Leagues Under the Sea*. London, Collins, 1974
Journey to the Centre of the Earth. London, Dent, 1970

Vipont, Elfrida and Briggs, R. *Elephant and the Bad Baby*. London, Hamilton, 1969

Walsh, Jill Paton. *The Emperor's Winding Sheet*. London, Macmillan, 1974

Webb, Kaye ed. *I Like This Poem; favourite poems chosen by children*. London, Penguin, 1979

Wells, H. G. *Time Machine*. London, Pan, 1960

Westall, Robert. *The Machine Gunners*. London, Macmillan, 1975

Wheels Go Round and *One Green Frog*. London, Methuen, 1981

White, E. B. *Charlotte's Web*. London, Hamilton, 1952

Wilder, Laura Ingalls. *Little House on the Prairie*. London, Methuen, 1970

Wildsmith, Brian. *ABC*. London, O.U.P. 1968

Williams, Jay. *The Practical Princesses and Other Liberating Fairy Tales*. London, Chatto, 1979

Williamson, Henry. *Tarka the Otter*. London, Bodley Head, 1978

Zindel, Paul. *My Darling My Hamburger*. London, Bodley Head, 1970
The Pigman. London, Bodley Head, 1969

Zion, Gene. *Harry the Dirty Dog*. London, Bodley Head, 1960

B. Books about Children's Books
The books listed were referred to in the text or used in the preparation of the book.

Alderson, Brian. *Catalogue of the exhibition of pictures by Maurice Sendak*. London, Bodley Head, 1976
Looking at Picture Books. London, National Book League, 1974

Aldiss, Brian. *The True History of Science Fiction*. New York, Doubleday, 1973

Armour, Jenny. *Take Off...* (Completely revised and expanded successor to *New Readers Start Here*) London, Library Association, 1980

American Library Association; Association for Library Service to Children and Young Adults. *Selecting Materials for Children and Young Adults; a bibliography of bibliographies and review sources*. Chicago, A.L.A., 1980

Aubrey, Irene E. *Sources of French-Canadian materials for children; bibliography*. Ottawa, National Library of Canada, 1977

Bader, Barbara. *American Picture Books from Noah's Ark to the Beast Within*. New York, Macmillan, 1976

Barto, Agnia. The Training of specialists for the production of books for children in Russia. *Bookbird*, vol. 13 no. 1 1975 pp. 10–66

Baskin, Barbara comp. *Notes for a Different Drummer; a guide to juvenile fiction portraying the handicapped*. Chicago, A.L.A., 1977

Bauer, Caroline Feller. *Handbook for Storytellers*. Chicago, A.L.A., 1977

Bernstein, Joanne ed. *Books to Help Children Cope With Separation and Loss*. New York, Bowker, 1977

Bettelheim, Bruno. *The Uses of Enchantment; the meaning and importance of fairy tales*. New York, Knopf, 1976

Binding, Paul. *Robert Louis Stevenson*. London, O.U.P., 1974

Blount, Margaret. *Animal Land; the creatures of children's fiction*. London, Hutchinson, 1974

British National Bibliography. London, British Library, cumulative

Brownhill, Sue comp. *Starting Point; books for the illiterate adult and older reluctant reader*. London, National Book League, 1979

Butler, Dorothy. *Babies Need Books*. London, Bodley Head, 1980

Cushla and Her Books. London, Hodder & Stoughton, 1979

Carlsen, G. Robert. *Books and the Teenage Reader; a guide for teachers, librarians and parents*. New York, Harper & Row, 2nd ed. 1980

Carlson, Ruth Kearney. *Emerging humanity; multi-ethnic literature for children and adolescents*. Duberque, Brown, 1972

Chambers, Nancy ed. *The Signal Approach to Children's Books*. London, Kestrel, 1980

Children's Books in Print. New York, Bowker, annual

Cianciolo, Patricia J. *Picture Books for Children*. Chicago, A.L.A., 2nd. ed. 1981

Colwell, Eileen. *Storytelling*. London, Bodley Head, 1980

Commire, Anne. *Something About the Author; facts and pictures about contemporary authors and illustrators of books for young people*. vol. 1. Detroit, Gale, 1971

Commonwealth Institute. *Commonwealth Children's Literature*. Checklists on Commonwealth Literature No. 1. London, Commonwealth Institute, 1979

Cook, Elizabeth. *The Ordinary and the Fabulous*. London, C.U.P., 1976

Crouch, Marcus and Ellis, Alec. *Chosen For Children; an account of the books which have been awarded the L.A. Carnegie Medal 1936–1975*. London, Library Association, 3rd. ed. 1977

Darton, F. J. Harvey. *Children's Books in England; five centuries of social life*. London, C.U.P., 1958

Dixon, Bob. *Catching Them Young*. 2 vols. London, Pluto Press, 1977

Dobler World Directory of Youth Periodicals. New York, Citation Press, 3rd. ed. 1970

Doctoral Dissertations on Children's Literature; *a catalogue of a selection of dissertations recently submitted to North American universities*. Ann Arbor, University Microfilms International, 1978

Elkin, Judith comp. *Multi-racial Books for the Classroom*; *a select list of children's books*. London, Library Association, Youth Libraries Group, 3rd. rev. ed. 1980

Ellis, Alec. *A History of Children's Reading and Literature*. London, Pergamon, 1968

Eliot, T. S. *Notes Towards the Definition of Culture*. London, Faber, 1948

Fader, Daniel and McNeill, Elton B. *Hooked On Books*. London, Pergamon, 1969

Fisher, Margery. *Intent Upon Reading*. London, Brockhampton, 1964

Matters of Fact; aspects of non-fiction for children. London, Brockhampton, 1972

Who's Who in Children's Books; a treasury of the familiar characters of childhood. London, Weidenfeld & Nicholson, 1975

Fletcher, Gordon R. and Jenkins, F. Books at work in Cleveland. *Assistant Librarian*. 70 (12) Dec. 1977 pp. 191–194

Foster, John L. *Reluctant to Read*. London, Ward Lock ed., 1977

Frend, Patricia M. ed. *Junior Fiction Index*. London, A.A.L., 3rd. ed. 1977

Frizzell Smith, Dorothy and Andrews, Eva L. *Subject Index to Poetry for Children and Young People, 1957–1975*. Chicago, A.L.A., 1977

Gardner, F. M. and Persson, L. C. comp. *Sequels*, vol. 2. *Junior Books*. London, A.A.L., 1976

Gersom, Diane ed. *Sexism and Youth*. New York, Bowker, 1974

Griffiths, Vivien and Barlow, Carole comp. *Ghostly Encounters*. Youth Libraries Group Pamphlet no. 19. London, Library Association, Youth Libraries Group, n.d.

Haviland, Virginia ed. *Children's Literature; views and reviews*. London, Bodley Head, 1974

Haviland, Virginia. *Children's Literature; a guide to reference sources*. Washington, Library of Congress, 1966. Supplement 1972

Hill, Janet. *Children are People; the librarian in the community*. London, Hamilton, 1973

Hotchkiss, Jeanette comp. *African-Asian Reading Guide*. Metuchen, Scarecrow, 1976

Hunt, Peter L. *Children's Book Research in Britain*. Cardiff, UWISS, Dept. of English, 1977

Hurlimann, Bettina. *Picture Book World*. London, O.U.P., 1967
  Three Centuries of Children's Books in Europe. edited and translated by Brian Alderson. London, O.U.P., 1967

Instituto Nacional del Libro Espanol. *Libros Infantiles y juveniles en España 1960–1975*. Madrid, Instituto Nacional del Libro Español, 1976

Interracial Books For Children Bulletin. vol. 7. no. 4. 1976

Issues in Children's Book Selection. New York, Bowker, 1974

Kemphes, Wolfgang. *International Bibliography of Comics Literature*. New York, Bowker, 2nd. rev. ed. 1974

Kennerley, Peter. *Running a School Bookshop; theory and practice*. London, Ward Lock Ed., 1978

Kingman, Lee and others. *Illustrators of children's books 1957–1966*. Boston, Hornbook, 1979

Kirkpatrick, D. L. comp *Twentieth Century Children's Writers*. London, Macmillan, 1978

Kloet, Christine A. comp. *After Alice; a hundred years of children's reading in Britain*. Catalogue of exhibition. London, Library Association, 1977

Kujoth, Jean Spealman. *Reading Interests of Children and Young Adults*. Metuchen, Scarecrow, 1970

Lane, Margaret. *The Tale of Beatrix Potter*. London, Warne, 1968

Lewis, C. S. On three ways of writing for children. In: Sheila Egoff et al. *Only Connect; readings on children's literature*. Toronto, O.U.P., 1969

Lewis, Naomi comp. *Fantasy Books For Children*. London, National Book League, 1977

Marshall, Margaret R. *Libraries and Literature for Teenagers*. London, Deutsch, 1975
  Libraries and the Handicapped Child. London, Deutsch, 1981

Seeing Clear; books for the partially sighted child. Oxford, School Library Association, 1977

Matsuoka, Kyoko. Feel it and read it; handmade books for handicapped children in Japan. *Bookbird.* no. 3 1980, pp. 26–27.

Meek, Margaret, and others, ed. *The Cool Web; the pattern of children's reading.* London, Bodley Head, 1977
Rosemary Sutcliff. London, Bodley Head, 1962

Meigs, Cornelia. *A Critical History of Children's Literature; a survey of children's books in English from earliest times to the present.* New York, Macmillan, rev. ed. 1970

Miller, Bertha Maloney and others. *Illustrators of Children's Books 1744–1945.* Boston, Hornbook, 1947

Monson, Dianne L. and Peltola, Bette J. *Research in Children's Literature; an annotated bibliography.* Newark, Del., International Research Association, 1976

Morris, Helen comp. *Where's That Poem?* London, Blackwell, 1979

Moss, Elaine. *Shirley Hughes* in *Signal.* May, 1980, pp. 21–22

Muir, Marcie. *Bibliography of Australian Children's Books.* London, Deutsch, vol. 1 1970, vol. 2, 1976

Newsletter on Intellectual Freedom. Chicago International Freedom Committee, A.L.A., bi-monthly

Patte, Geneviève. *Laissez-les Lire; les enfants et les bibliothèques.* Paris, Ed. Ouvrières, 1978

Pellowski, Anne. *Made to Measure; children's books in developing countries.* Paris, Unesco, 1980 (in French, Spanish and English editions)
The World of Children's Literature. New York, Bowker, 1968
The World of Storytelling. London & New York, Bowker, 1977

Polette, Nancy and Mamlin, Marjorie. *Exploring Books With Gifted Children.* New York, Libraries Unlimited, 1980

Ray, Colin comp. *Background to Children's Books.* London, National Book League, 4th. ed. 1977

Ray, Colin ed. *Library Service to Children; an international survey of 21 countries*. Munich, Verlag Dokumentation. New York, K. G. Saur, 1978

Ray, Sheila. *The Blyton Phenomenon*. London, Deutsh, 1982

Children's Fiction. London, Brockhampton, 1970

Roberts, Lorna. *The 1979 Bookmaster Scheme*. London, Westminster City Libraries, 1979

Salway, Lance ed. *A Peculiar Gift*; (essays on nineteenth century children's book authors). London, Penguin, 1976

St. John, Judith. *The Osborne Collection; early children's books 1566–1910; a catalogue*. Toronto, Toronto Public Library, 1958. vol. 2. 1976

Saxby, Maurice ed. *Through Folklore to Literature*; papers presented at the Australian National Section of IBBY Conference on children's literature 1978. Sydney, IBBY Australian Publications, 1979

Scherf, Walter. comp. *The Best of the Best; picture, children's and youth books from 110 countries or languages*. Munich, Verlag Dokumentation, 2nd. ed. 1976

School Bookshop Association. *How To Set Up and Run a Schoolbookshop*. London, School Bookshop Association, 1981

Scott, Dorothea Hayward. *Chinese Popular literature and the Child*. Chicago, A.L.A., 1980

Stinton, Judith ed. *Racism and sexism in children's books; facts, figures and guidelines*. London, Writers and Readers Publications Group, 1980

Stratford, Brian and Maureen. *Fiction for the Slow Reader*. London, National Book League, 1981

Subero, Efrain. *La Literature Infantil Venezuelana; estudio y bibliografica*. Caracas, Centro de Cepacitacian Docente de El Macaro, 1972

Subject Guide to Children's Books In Print. New York, Bowker, current.

Sutherland, Zena and Arbuthnot, May Hill. *Children and Books*. New York, Scott, Foresman, 5th. ed. 1975

Townsend, John Rowe. *Written For Children*. London, Kestrel, 1974

Tucker, Nicholas. *Suitable For Children; controversies in children's literature*. Brighton, Sussex University Press, 1976

Tuill, P. Little Black Sambo; the continuing controversy. *School Library Journal*, 22 (7) March 76 pp. 71–75.

Turow, Joseph. *Getting Books to Children; an exploration of publisher–market relations*. A.L.A. Studies in Librarianship no. 7. Chicago, A.L.A., 1978

Unesco; Division for Book Promotion and Encouragement of International Cultural Exchanges. *Children and Books*. I.Y.C. Discussion Paper. Paris, Unesco, 1979

Unesco; Regional Centre for Book Development in Asia. *Final Report of the Regional Seminar* on planning, production and distribution of books for children and young people in Asia. Karachi, Unesco Regional Centre, 1975

Viguers, Ruth Hill and others. *Illustrators of Children's Books, 1946–1958*. Boston, Hornbook, 1968

Watts, Lynne and Nisbet, J. *Legibility in Children's Books*. London, N.F.E.R. 1974

Wehmeyer, Lillian Biermann. *Images in a Crystal Ball; world futures in novels for young people*. New York, Libraries Unlimited, 1982

Wertheimer, Leonard ed. Library services to ethno-cultural minorities. *Library Trends*, Fall 29 (2) 1980

Whitehead, Frank and others. *Children and Their Books*. Schools Council Project. London, Macmillan, 1977

Wilkinson, Donald. *Information Books for the Slow Reader*. London, National Book League, 1979

C. Select List of Children's Literature Periodicals

BOOKBIRD quarterly IBBY and The International Institute for Children's Literature and Reading Research, Vienna

BOOKLIST twice a month American Library Association, Chicago

BOOKS FOR KEEPS 6 times a year School Bookshop Association, London

BOOK REVIEW DIGEST 10 times a year, Wilson, New York

BRITISH BOOK NEWS monthly and quarterly children's book supplement British Council, London

BULLETIN OF THE CENTER FOR CHILDREN'S BOOKS monthly Center for Children's Books, Chicago

CHILDREN'S BOOK BULLETIN 3 times a year. Children's Rights Workshop, London

CHILDREN'S LITERATURE ABSTRACTS quarterly IFLA Colin Ray, 45, Stephenson Tower, Station Street, Birmingham, UK

CHILDREN'S LITERATURE IN EDUCATION 3 times a year, Agathon Press, New York

CHILDREN'S LITERATURE REVIEW twice a year, Gale, Detroit

GROWING POINT 9 times a year, Margery Fisher, Ashton Manor, Northampton, UK

HORNBOOK MAGAZINE 6 times a year, Hornbook Inc., Boston, USA

JUNIOR BOOKSHELF 6 times a year, Marshall Hall, Thurstonland, Huddersfield, UK

LA REVUE DES LIVRES POUR ENFANTS 6 times a year, La Joie Par les Livres, Paris

LIBRARY AND INFORMATION SCIENCE ABSTRACTS (LISA) quarterly, Library Association, London

LIBRARY LITERATURE (Abstracts) quarterly

PHAEDRUS; an international journal of children's literature research, quarterly, James Fraser PO Box 1166 Marblehead, Mass., USA

RADIALS BULLETIN twice a year, Library Association, London

READING quarterly, International Reading Association, London

REVIEW quarterly. School Libraries Branch of the Education Department of South Australia, Adelaide

SCHOOL LIBRARIAN quarterly, School Library Association, Oxford

SCHOOL LIBRARY JOURNAL monthly, Sept–May Bowker, New York

SIGNAL 3 times a year, Thimble Press, Stroud, UK

TOP OF THE NEWS monthly, Children's Services Division, American Library Association, Chicago.

Index

References to names of countries cover the children's literature, libraries and organizations of the country.

183